Love Rhymes with Everything

Love Rhymes
with Everything

Animal ruminations
through poetry & paintings

Art by Dana Feagin

Poetry by Kat von Cupcake

Ashland
Creek
Press

Love Rhymes with Everything
Animal ruminations through poetry & paintings

Published by Ashland Creek Press
Ashland, Oregon
www.ashlandcreekpress.com

ISBN 978-1-61822-052-3
Library of Congress Control Number: 2016963489

Printed in the United States of America on acid-free paper.
All paper products used to create this book are Sustainable Forestry Initiative
(SFI) Certified Sourcing.

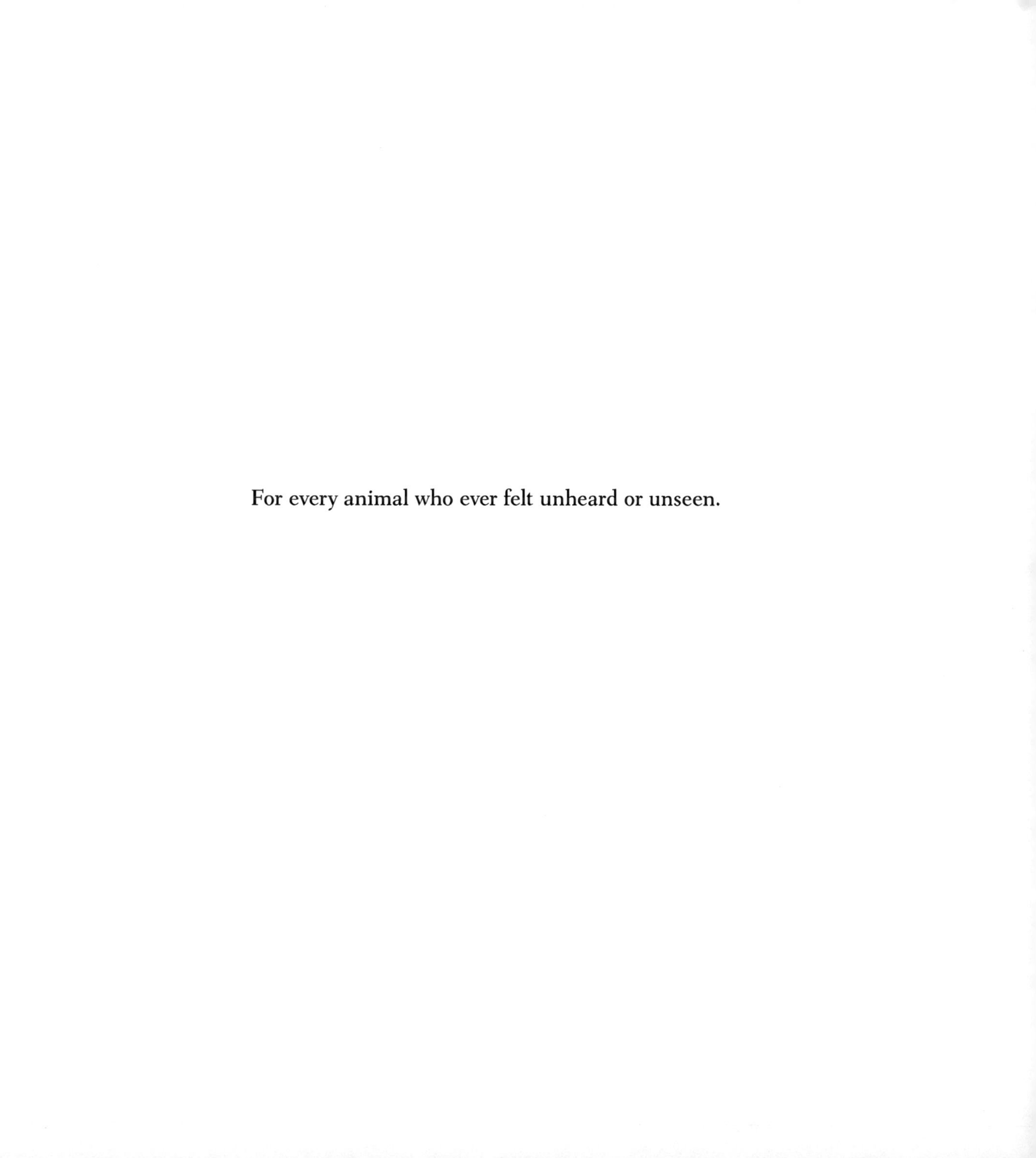

For every animal who ever felt unheard or unseen.

Foreword

The animals with whom we share this planet have countless stories to tell. The only problem is that we speak different languages (most of the time). Yet it is so important—even when we think we can't understand our fellow creatures—that we listen and observe. So much that gets lost in translation is, in fact, right in front of us—if we pay close attention.

Dana Feagin and Kat von Cupcake are among those who are listening, and they have much to share with us.

Dana's lovely, whimsical paintings have been hanging in Ashland galleries for nearly a decade. And it was at Dana's art show at a Sanctuary One fundraiser that I first met Kat, over a platter of her vegan cupcake minis. Always a fan of Dana and Kat's talents, I'm also incredibly fortunate to call them both friends.

And Dana and Kat, who both serve on the board of Sanctuary One, are friends of the animals in so many ways. They give their time, their passion, and their artistic gifts—and they are generously donating all proceeds of this book to sanctuaries and rescues.

I've had the privilege of meeting many of the animals featured in this book—the horses of Equamore; the farm animals of Sanctuary One; Kat's own Little Inez and Bella; Dana's Riley, Oscar, Nell, and Chive—and Theo, the general manager of Ashland Creek Press and our family cat for the past seventeen years. It's wonderful to see these animals—so many of them formerly abused or abandoned—honored in paintings and poetry.

Rescued animals have sad stories, but the animals you'll meet in this book are the lucky ones; they ended up at shelters and sanctuaries, where they will live out their lives in peace or be adopted to loving homes. *Love Rhymes with Everything* ensures that all of them will be remembered, as will the humans who have loved them and cared for them.

The poems and paintings collected here remind us that all animals have unique personalities, stories, and histories. And, thanks to Dana, Kat, and all of you who are reading and sharing this book, more animals will have hopeful futures as well.

Midge Raymond
February 2017
Ashland, Oregon

Ambassador

I am the one
you will most likely see
when you arrive at the gate
of the sanctuary

In the front-most pasture
I wait to meet
the visitors who come
they are all mine to greet

I am all snorts and smiles
as I escort you through the gate
Just look at my life now!
Isn't it great?

For my name is Lulu
and I am the start of your tour
I think this is why folks call me
the ambassador

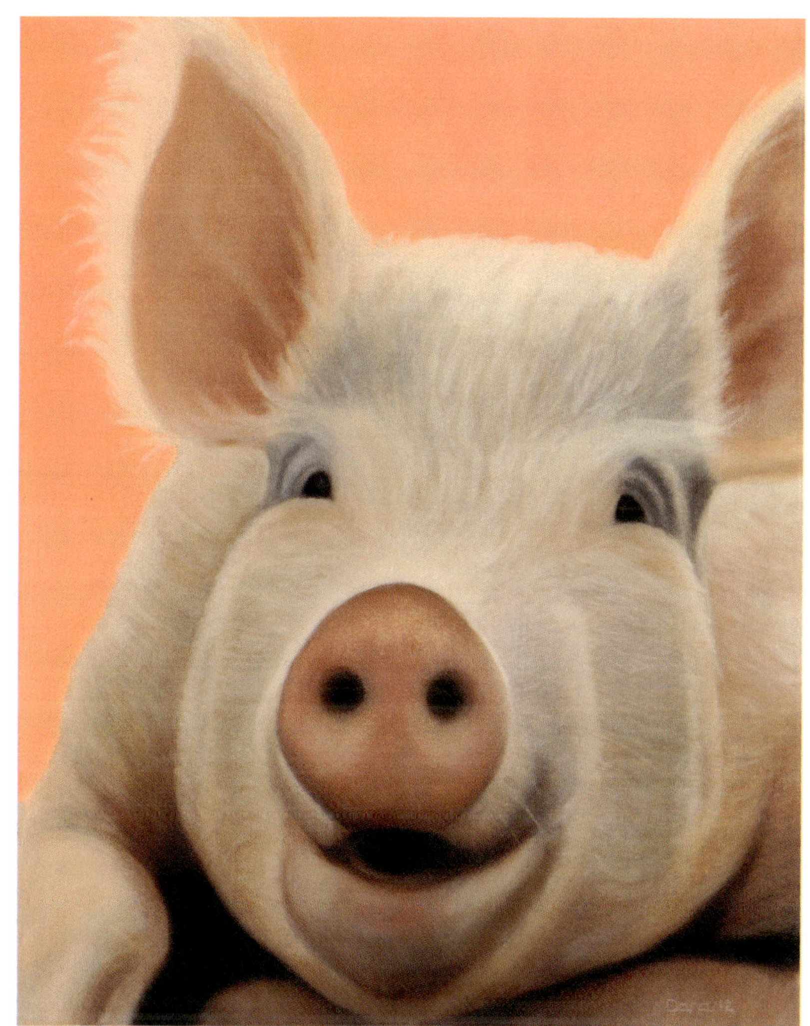

Ode to a Ball

Have you seen my red ball?
Because I don't see it at all.

I woke up from my nap;
now all I see is a gap
where my ball used to be;
oh, woe is me.

Yes, I looked over there
and underneath the blue chair;
no red did I see.
Are you laughing at me?

Soon my dinner will call
so please do not tease;
come on, my dear human,
and find my red ball.

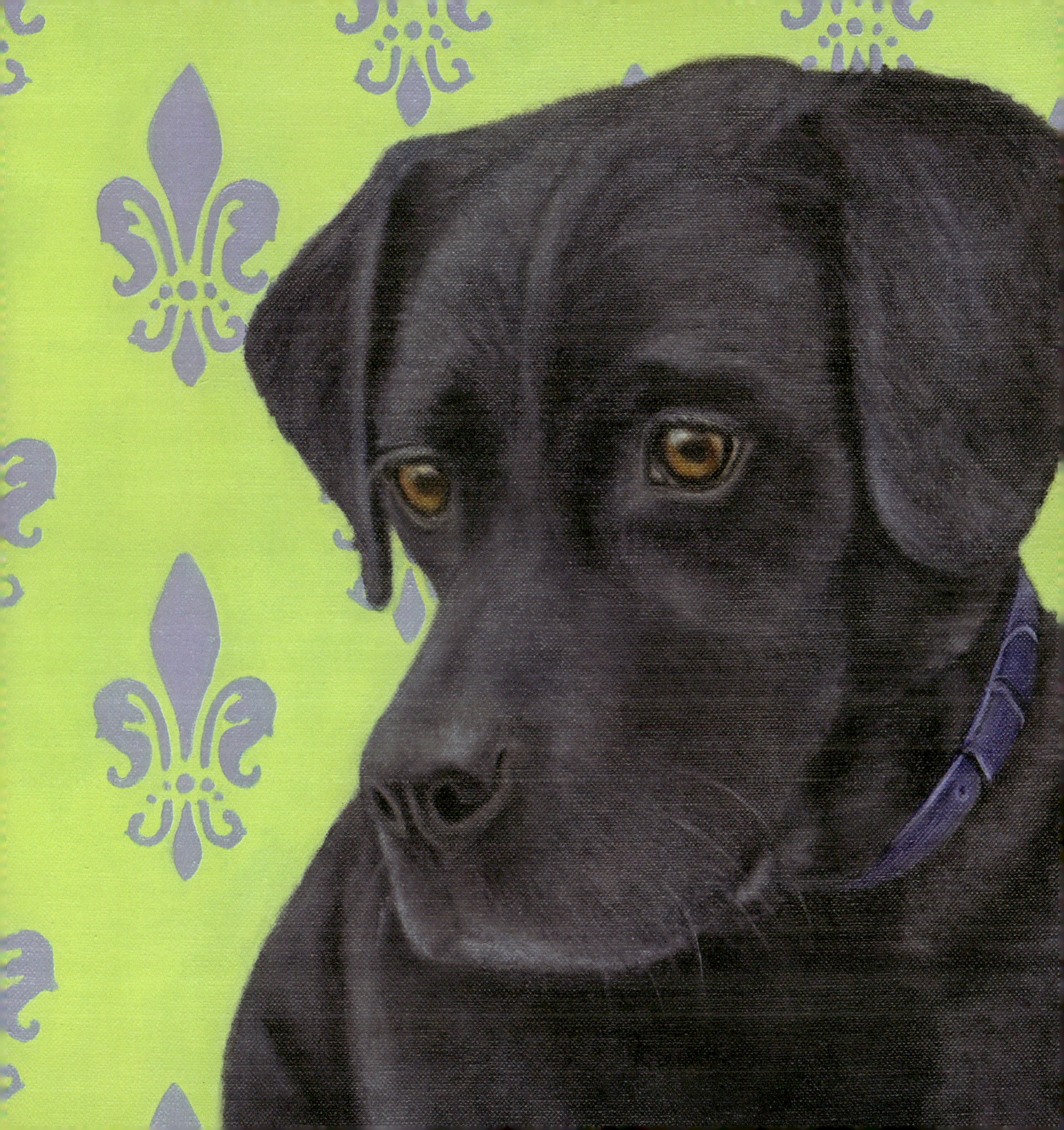

Wardrobe Malfunction

Hey!
Hey you—
over there—
oops, sorry,
didn't mean to scare
and not that you care,
but I think I should share
and make you aware
that when you came out of there,
your skirt—it got tucked into
your pink underwear.

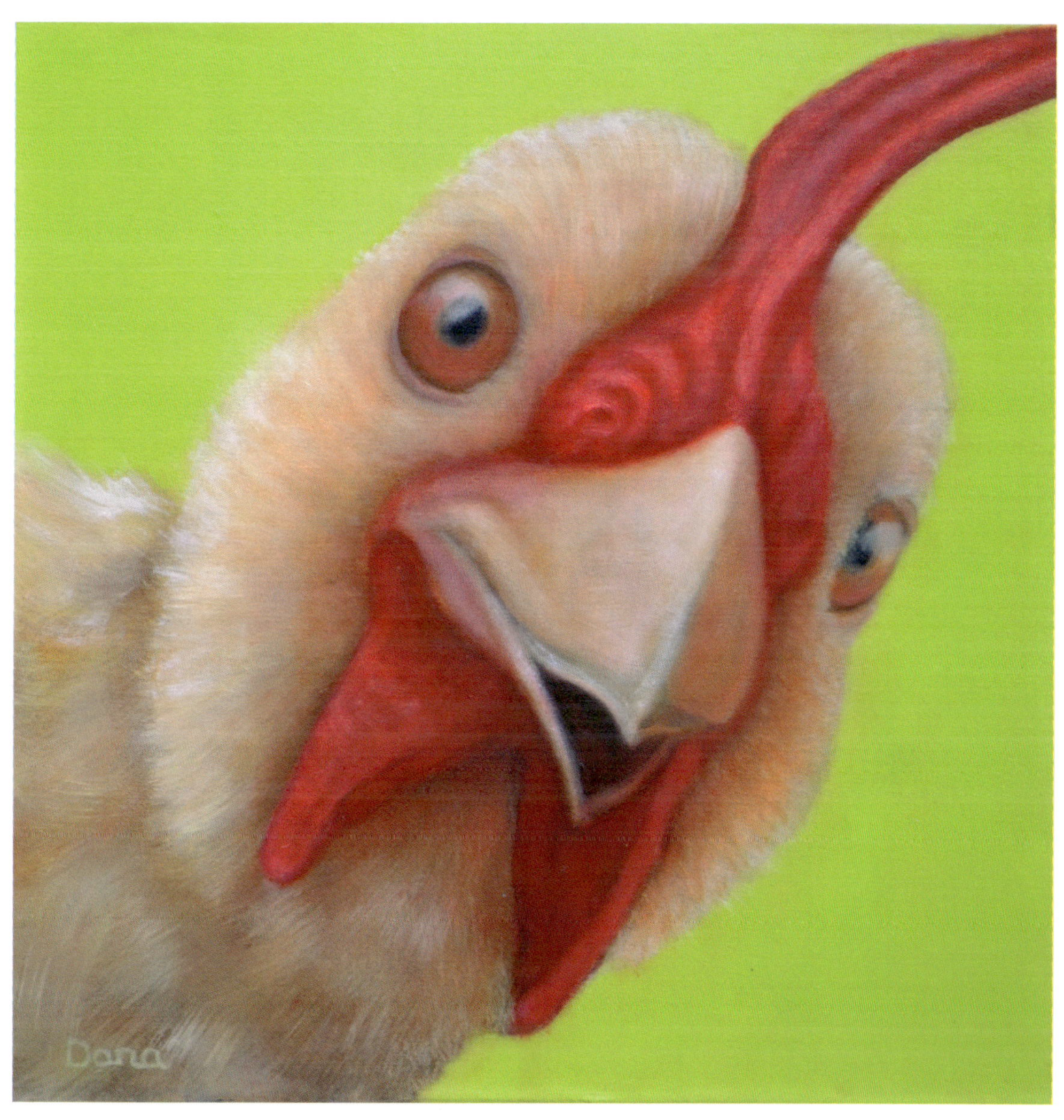
Dana

Maynard
Loves Brian

He is sitting on the bench
he is right over there
it's that man I call friend
I can tell by his hair

I hop up beside him
and then to his lap
and then my long neck
around his I wrap

My focus is pulled
and I begin eyeing
those shoes on his feet
they beg for untying

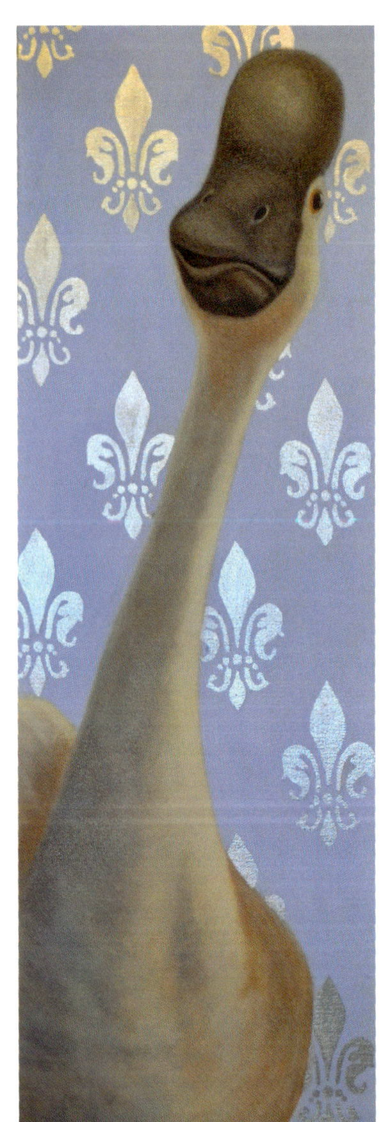

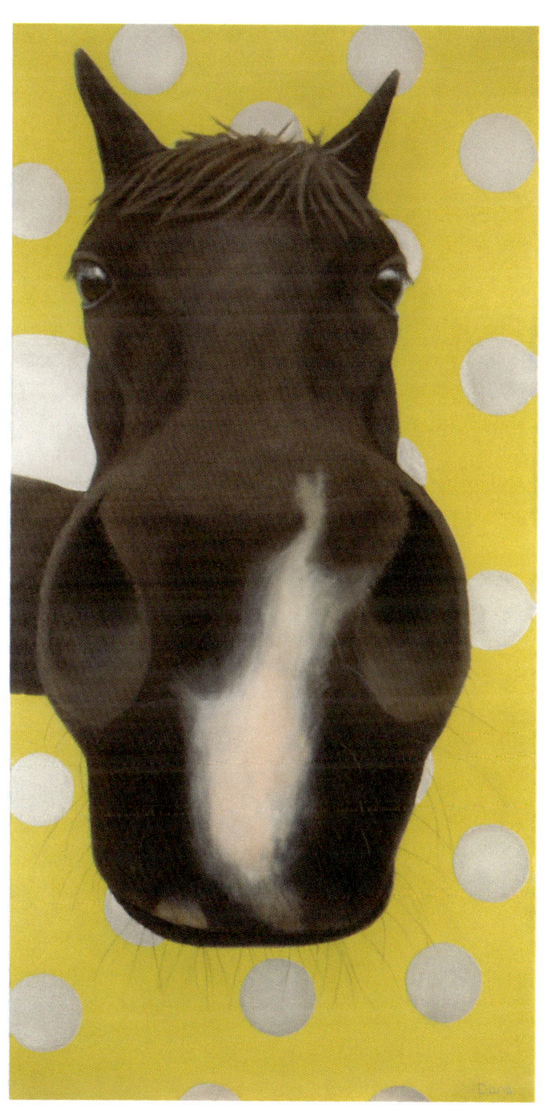

No Words

This one is too hard
I just can't write it
every time I begin
my breaking heart fights it

the way you were treated
it should be a crime
neglect so severe
unforgivable, unkind

sanctuaries and rescues
our need for them soars
in your case sweet Chaps
bless the hearts of Equamore

your ending is happy
not all of them are
you made it through hell
just show them your scar

Stare Down

I won't blink
if you won't.

I won't move
if you don't.

You think you're so clever,
but I can do this forever.

You give up?
Whatever.

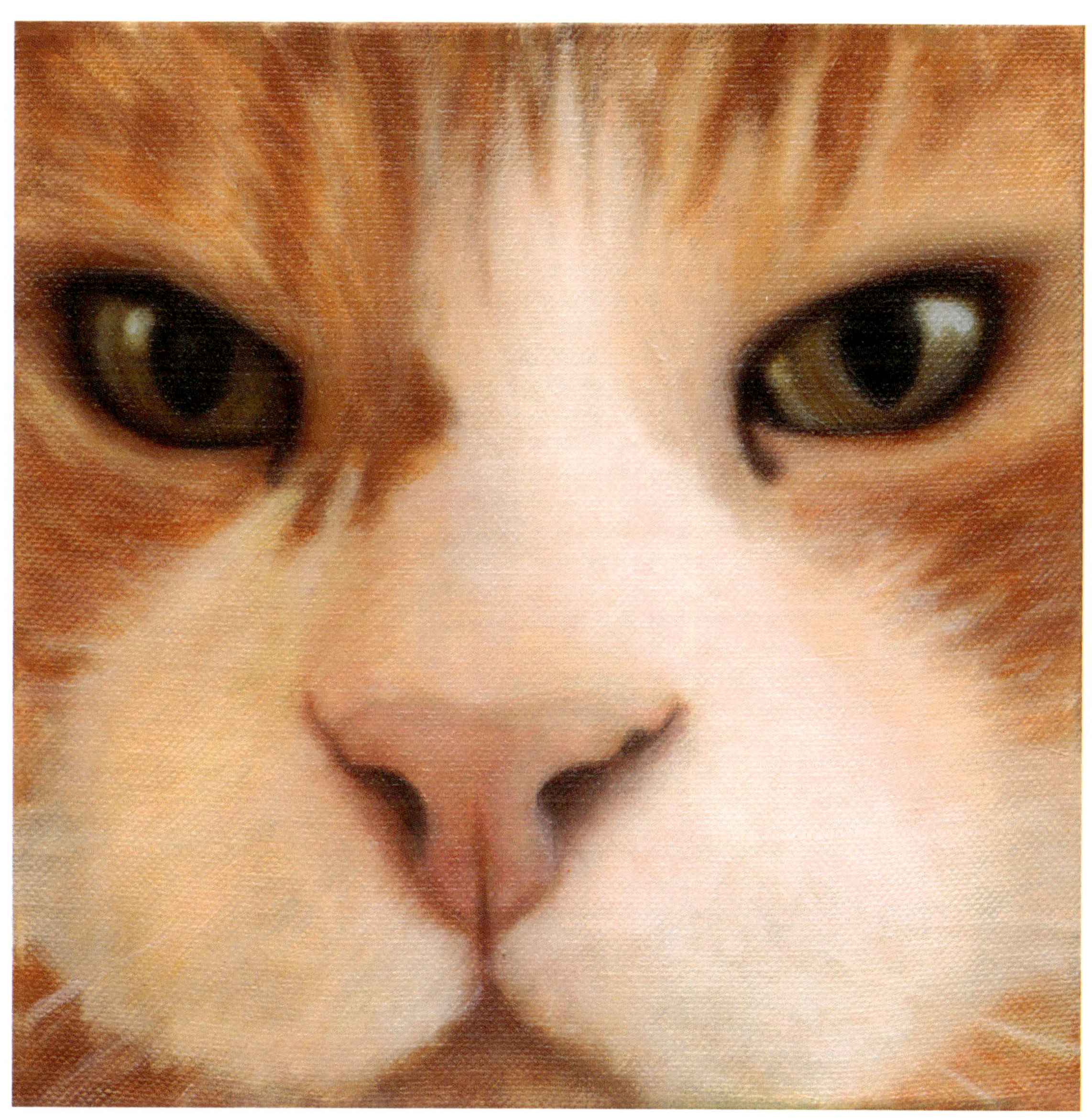

Farm Gossip

I just heard from Stan,
you know the man,
that the black cat from the barn
got caught with the yarn
that Stan's wife named Hester
used to knit her "friend" Lester
a nice Christmas sweater
to make him feel better.

The cat didn't know
that the sweater really showed
Hester's feelings for Lester
since Easter had grown.
Now Stan is quite mad
and feels like a cad
that he had not seen
what the yarn the cat had
really might mean.

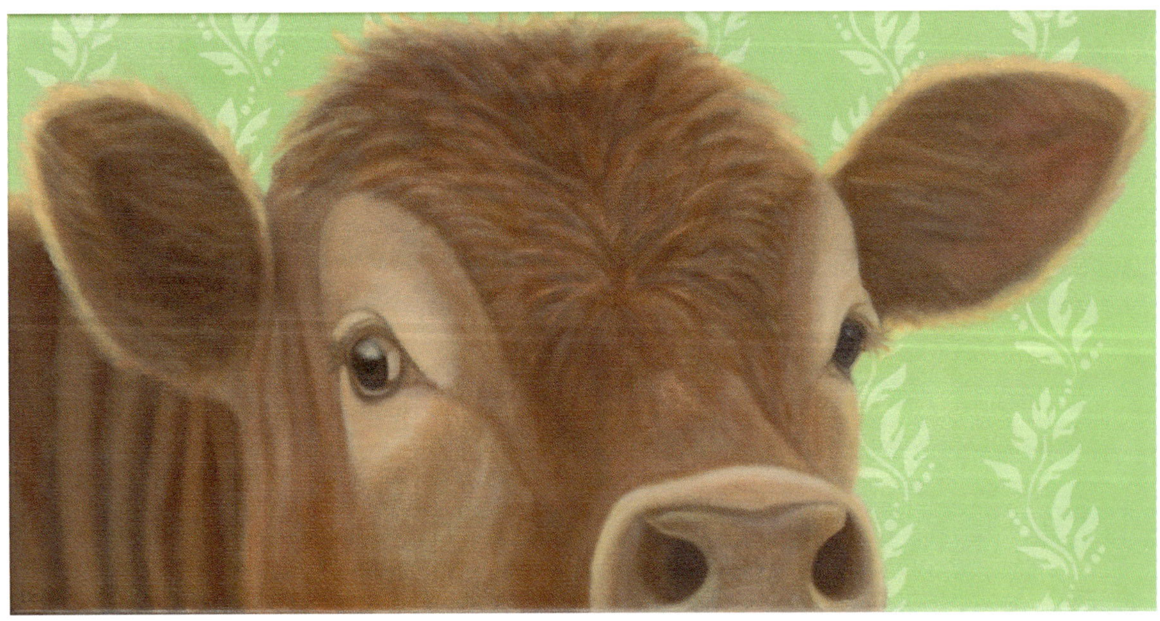

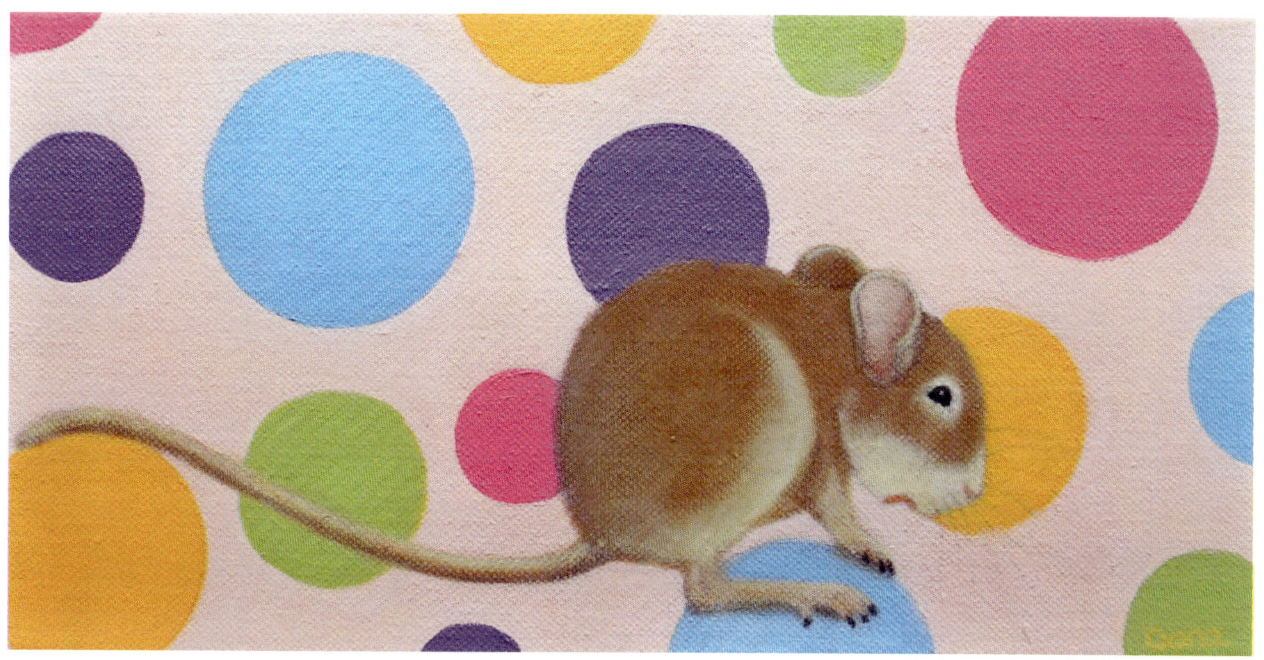

Out of the Blue

I live in the field
behind the big bright blue house
It looks like a bubble
through the eyes of a mouse

I sometimes sneak in
when I need a quick snack
but I have to be careful
the house cat can track

Scamper and weave
bob up, duck down low
in the kitchen I spy
a fluffy marshmallow

Something is afoot!
Is that a furry paw that I see?
Next an unexpected friend
is offering a marshmallow to me.

Eau de Boxer

Some girls like sweaters,
but I find them too tight.
Some prefer pretty collars,
but they must fit just right.

The boys like a nice
bandanna to wear,
but I find them too butch,
and for that I'm too fair.

I say what the heck
if I want to wear
a strand of pretty flowers
around my sweet neck.

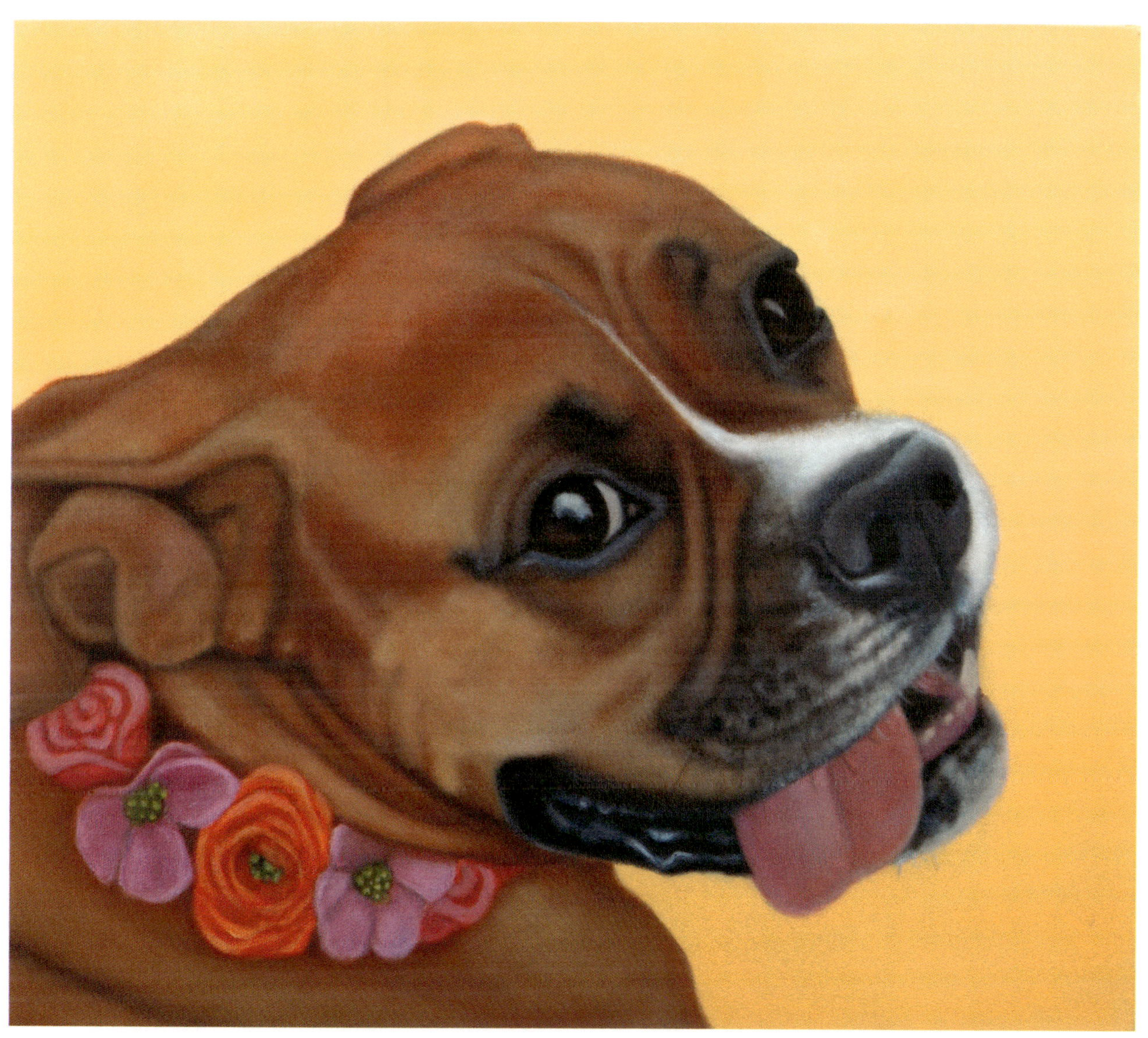

small dog, big hat

my brothers and sisters
are laughing at me
just one photo you said,
how cute it will be!

you would never think
to try this with the cat,
never force him to wear
this ridiculous hat

focus that lens
your window is narrow,
cuz imma start chewin'
this giant sombrero

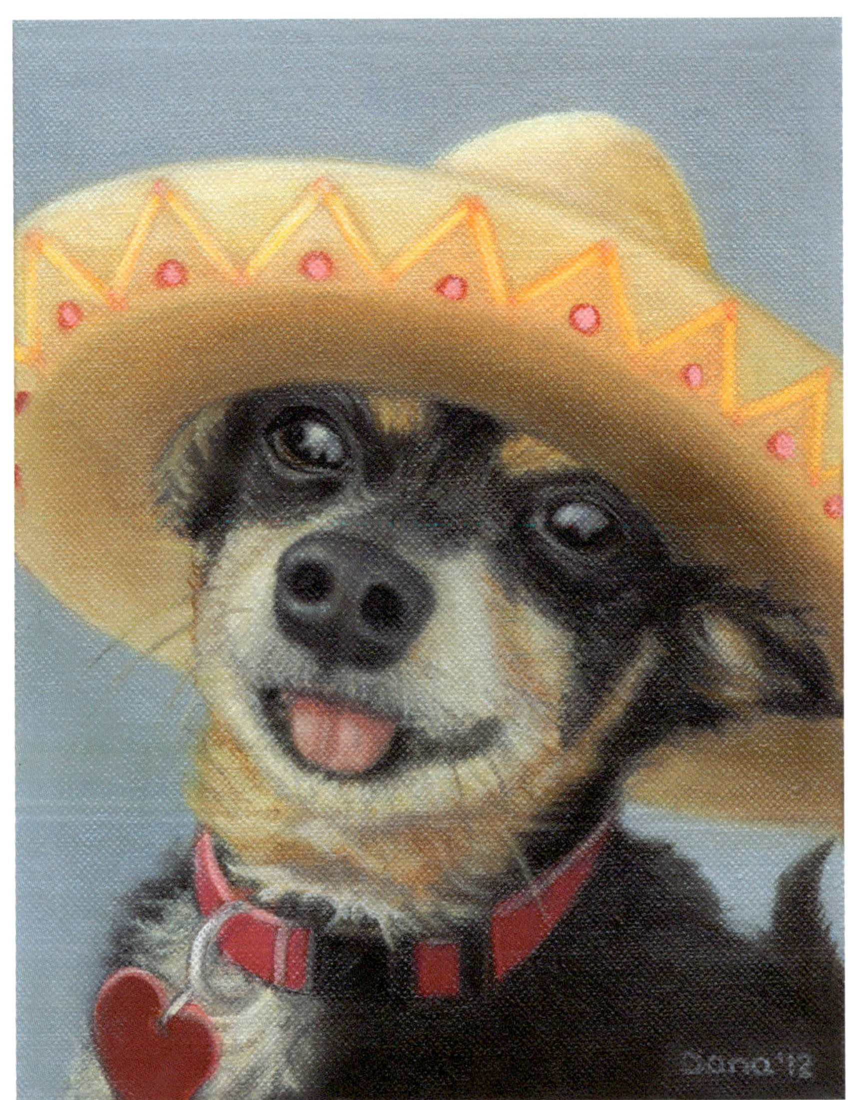

Goat Power

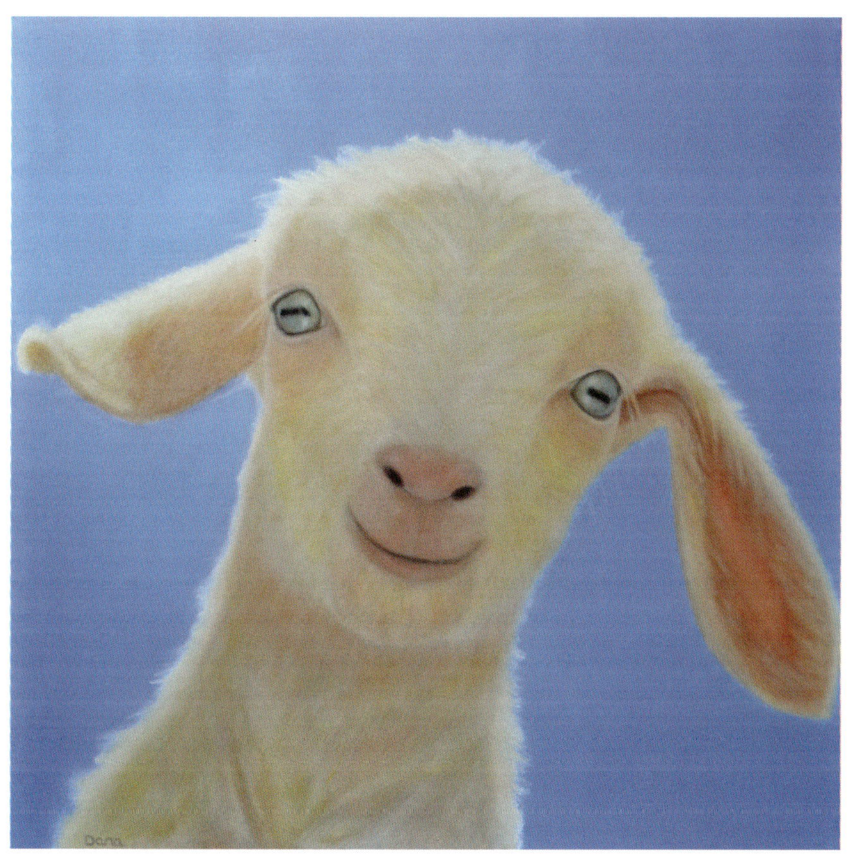

Some see me
and think what a cutie
and assume that being cute
is my only duty

some see me and think
of fresh milk & cheeses
or in the nativity
near the tiny baby jesus

but really us goats
we are so much more
we are dwarf and lamancha
and some of us boer

I know I may look
like a delicate flower,
but do not underestimate
my immense caprine power

It's a Pitty

All the false accusations
and myths aren't true.
How would you feel
if people hated you?

My jaws are no different,
no intricate locks.
I can prove it to you;
let me chew on your socks.

My heart is as loving
as any other breed.
So please, fearful humans,
stop planting these seeds.

We sit in the shelters
much longer than most
feeling invisible
like sad, love-starved ghosts.

Pit bulls are one of
life's wonderful treats,
so pet me and love me
instead of crossing the street.

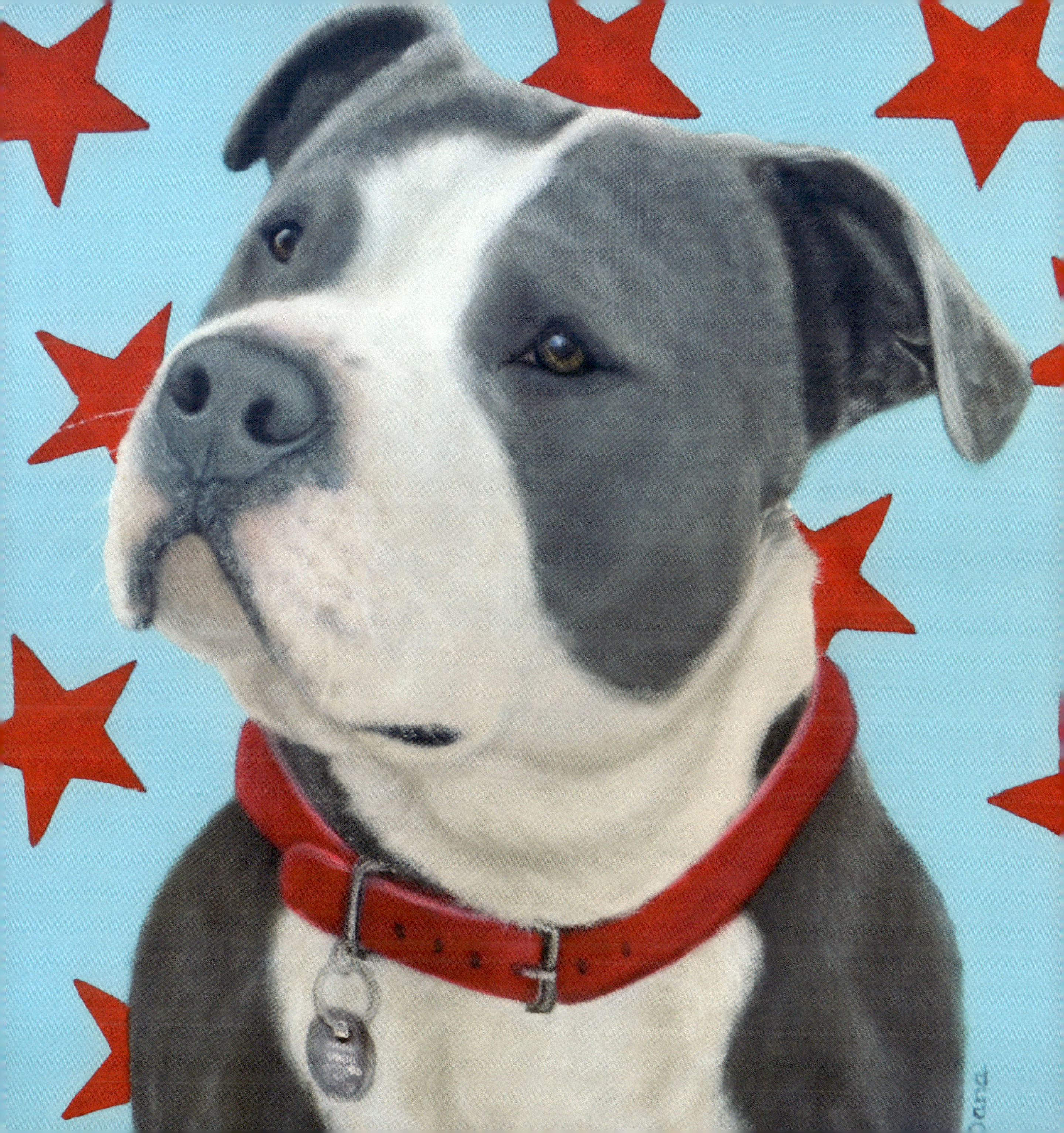

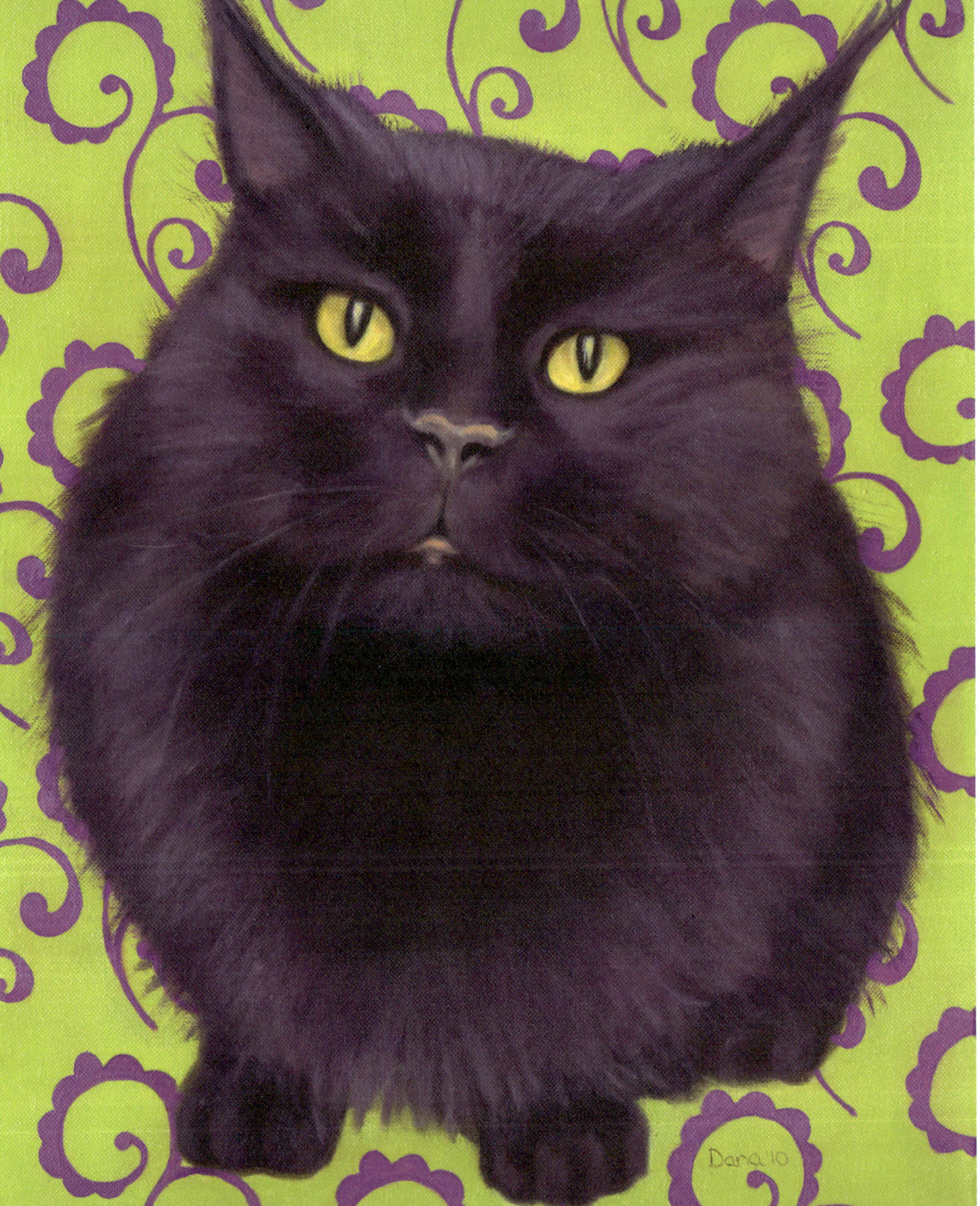
Dana '10

fuzz patrol

look at you with your magical stick
rolling it on everything
first pass slow
next pass quick

every morning
without fail
weapon in hand
over upholstery you prevail

you glance at me
with only half a smile
muttering about my hair
all the while

peel and tear
I don't care
because I am gonna rub my body
everywhere

N not M

When stating my breed,
pronunciation is key.
If I were a cat,
you wouldn't call me Sianese.

My breed is specific,
so get it right please.
I do not hail from Burma
so don't call me Burmese.

There is no need to tease;
just pronounce the word.
It sounds like cold legs.
You get it?
Burrrrrrr knees

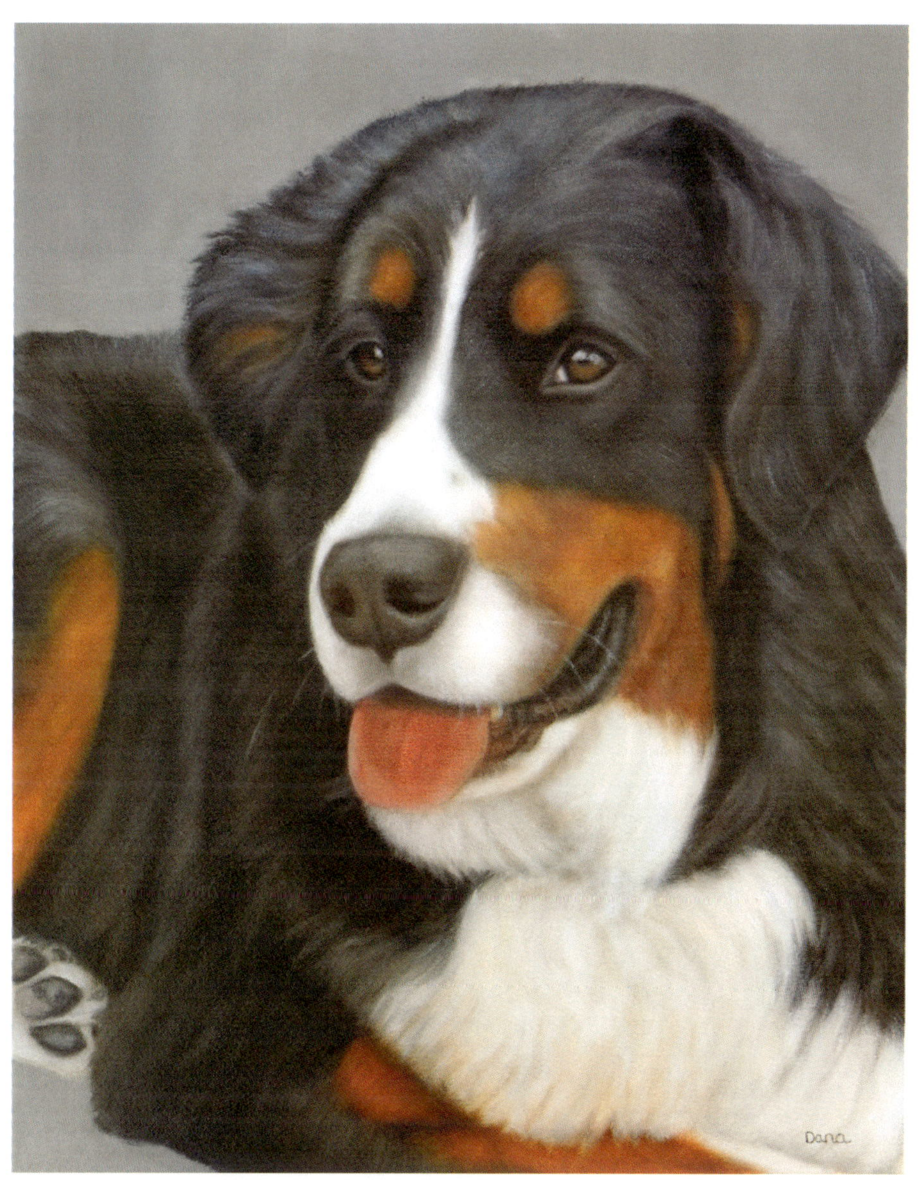

Dana

¿Como se Llama?

My job it requires
a keen sense of intuition;
there are others you could hire,
but your expectations
would not come to fruition.

Your herd needs a guardian
who is always alert,
so why would you not
call in an expert?

My vigilance is real;
my dedication you will feel.
I will guard your alpacas
(with my ears shaped like commas)
'cause predators know
not to mess with the llamas.

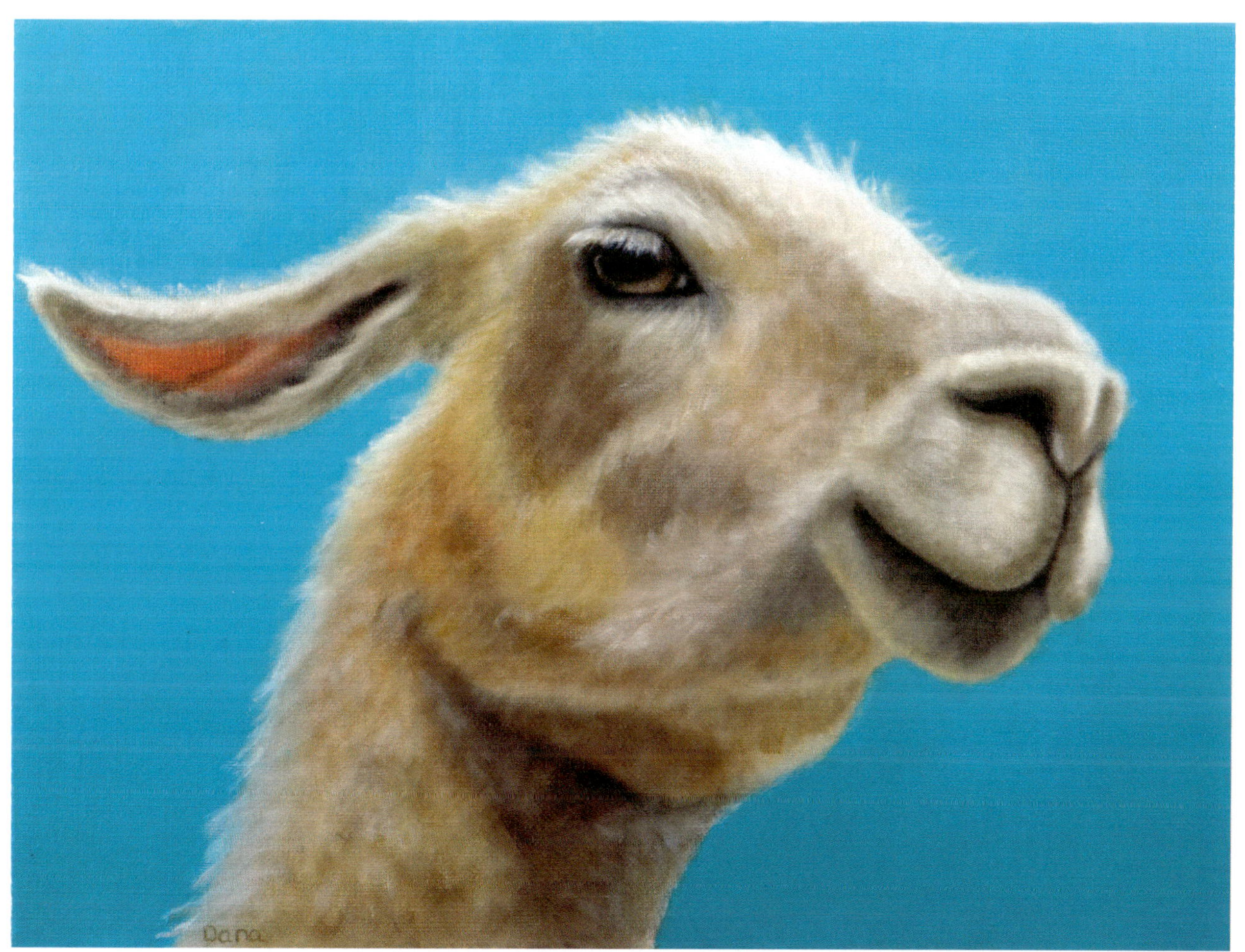

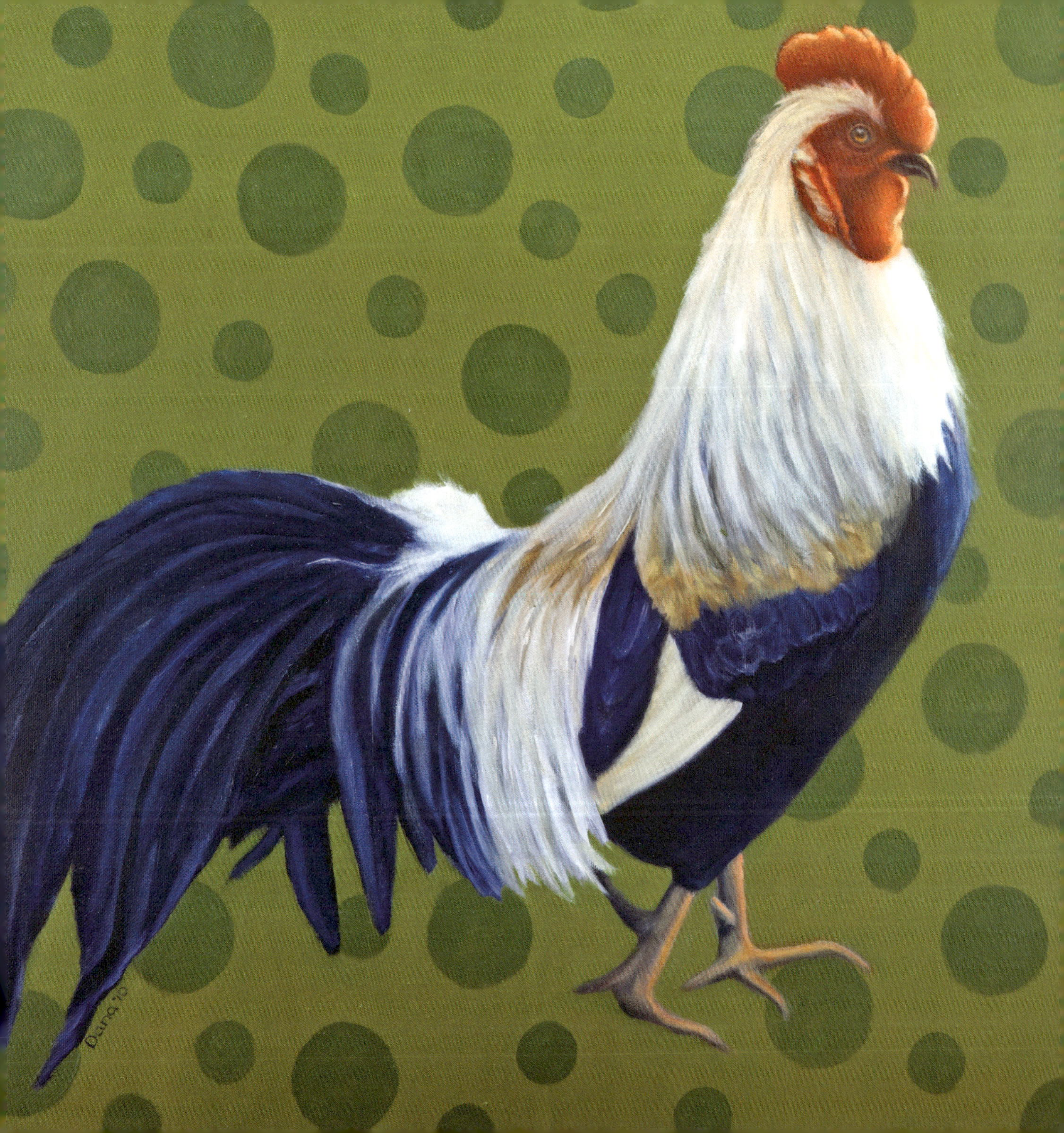

Next Dance

It should come as no shock
that I walk the walk.
For I am a rooster
(I prefer rooster to cock).

Folks look at me
and think: Oh, how pretty!
Upon closer inspection,
I make even myself giddy.

All of these antics,
why I preen so and prance.
What I am trying to say is:
Would you care to dance?

A Star Is Born

Diamonds in the sky
were Lucy's pure luck.
But all 'round *my* head,
giant stars have been stuck.

In this big, beautiful world
I haven't a care,
because love truly is
soft as an easy chair.

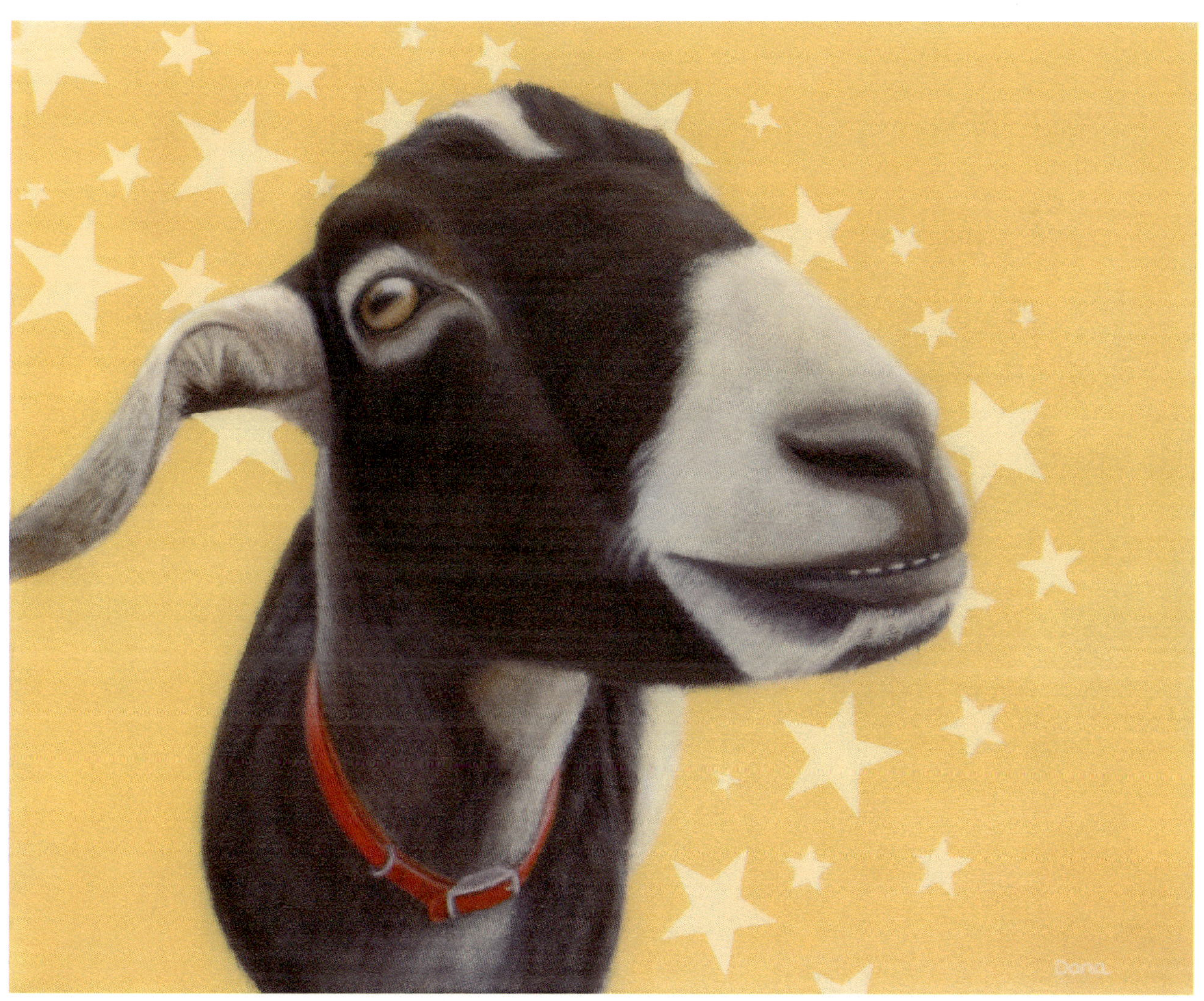

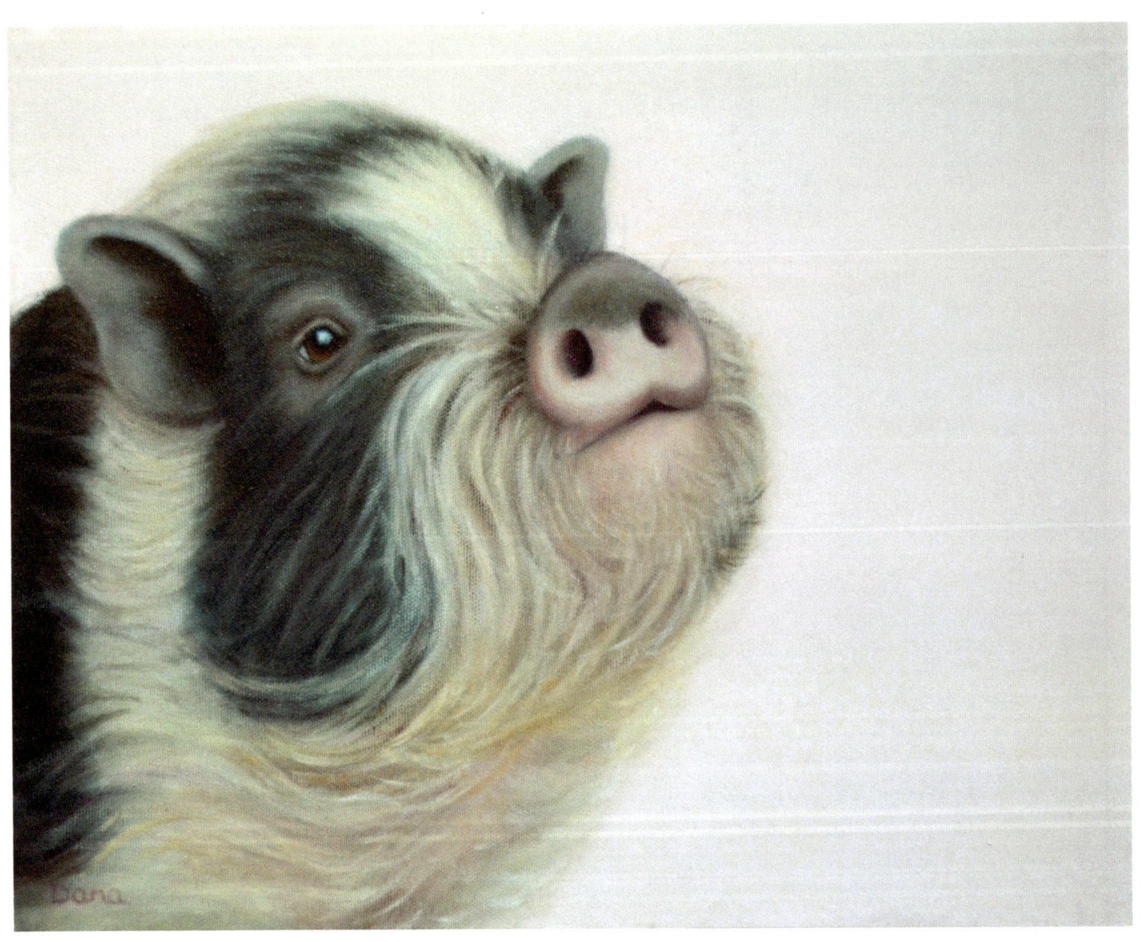

Cartman Likes Pie

Yes that was a sigh
'cause I thought I smelled pie
It was in the air
I swear
It just tickled my chin hair

My nose says it's berry
or possibly cherry
my nose always knows
just ask my pal Larry

From the field I can see it
it is out on the sill
to cool and to taunt me
could that be pumpkin I smell?

no joyrides

hey jack!
get off my back
what makes you think
I want to feel your butt crack

how would you feel
if folks jumped on you
and rode you around
instead of walking on the ground

do you think it's okay that
into my sides your heels jab
if you want transportation
go call a cab

science has proven
the pain that it brings
so quit with the riding
of other living things

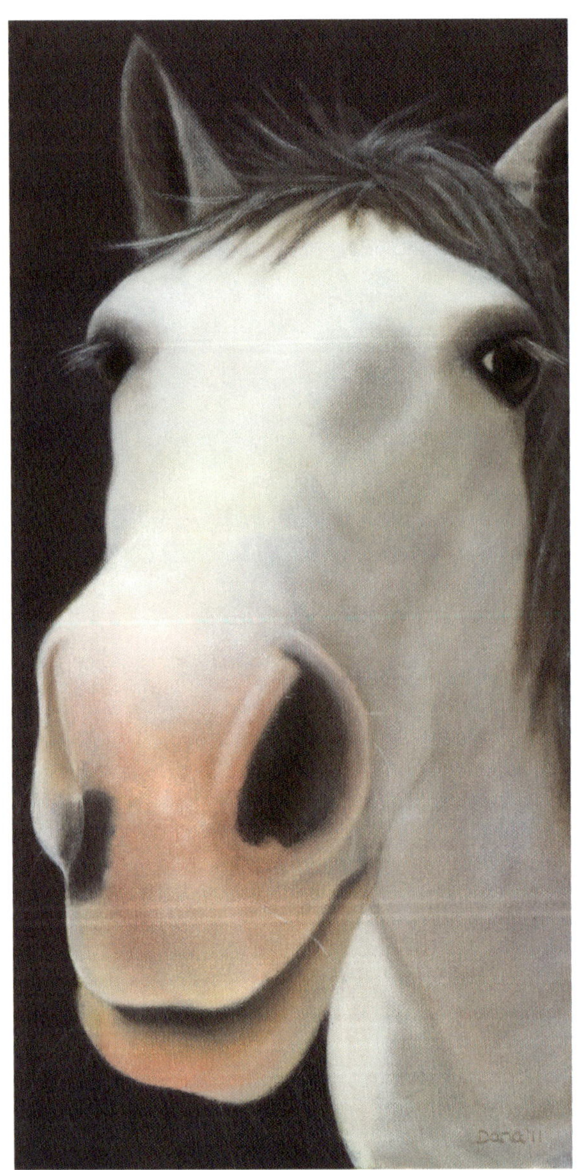

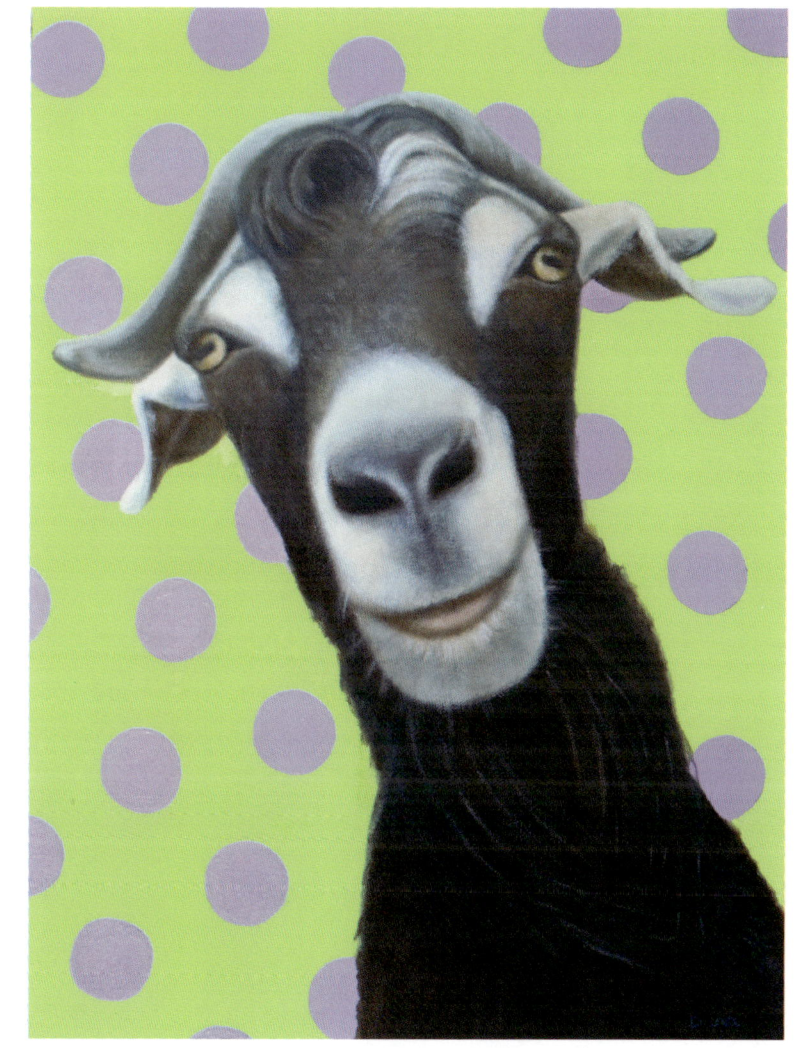

Django

I made it
I am here
No more fear
No more pain
Best of all
Good-bye chain

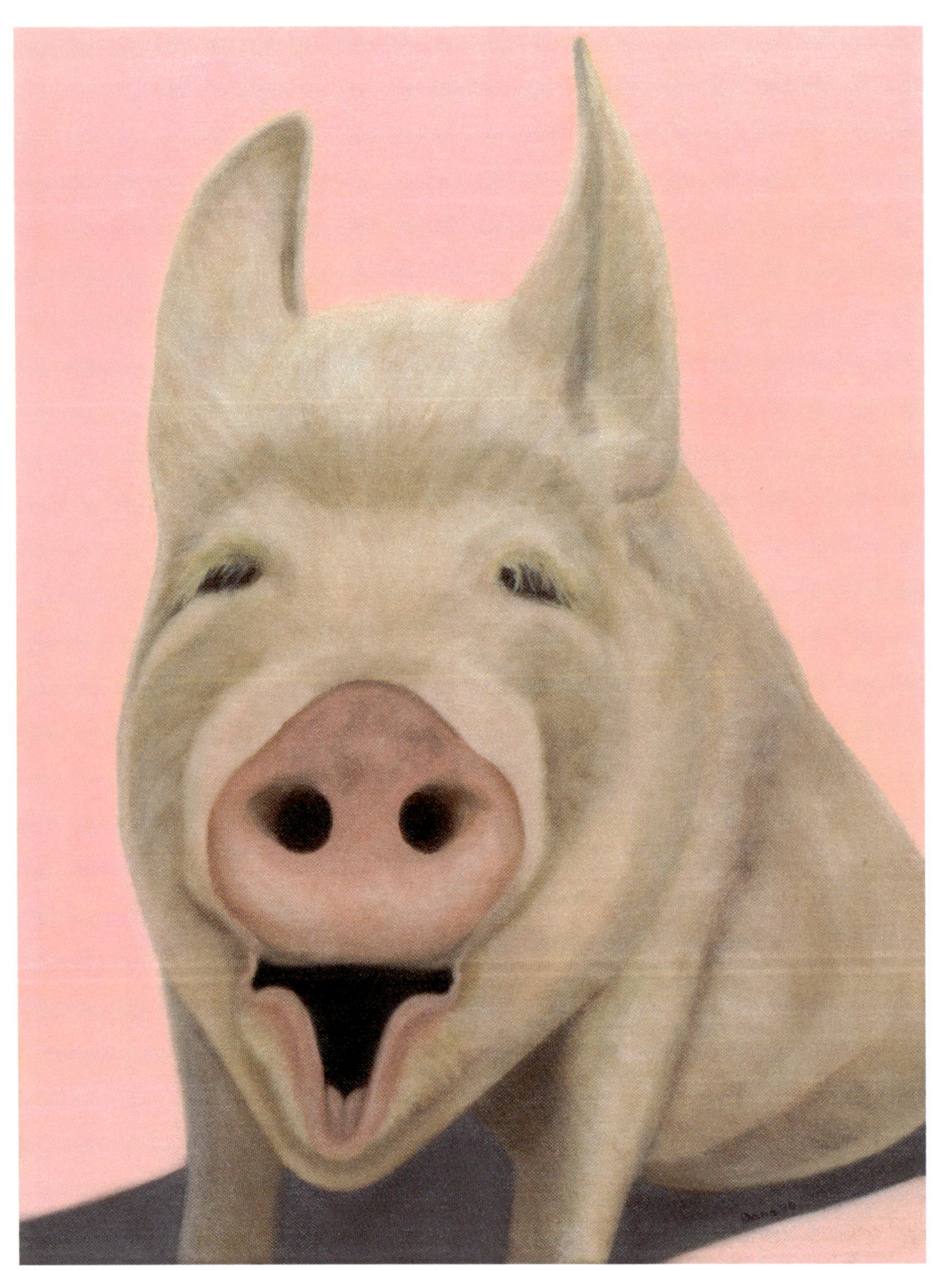

Goodnight Sansa

Let's laugh!
Don't be sad.
Let's smile and remember
all the great times
we have had.

This place is so peaceful
no street lights
no cars
just you my dear friend
a beer
and the stars

I inhale deeply
this is my last breath
thanks to you
I fear nothing
not even my death

Ar-teest

Those paintings I saw,
I couldn't help but stare.
Sweet animal faces, big eyes,
the artist's pure care.

She painted horses and dogs
and goaties, oh wow.
But my favorite that day
was a pink polka dot cow.

I sent her a letter
and spilled how I felt—
that the works she created
made my heart melt.

And now, five years later,
a friendship it took.
Her paintings, my words
together in a book.

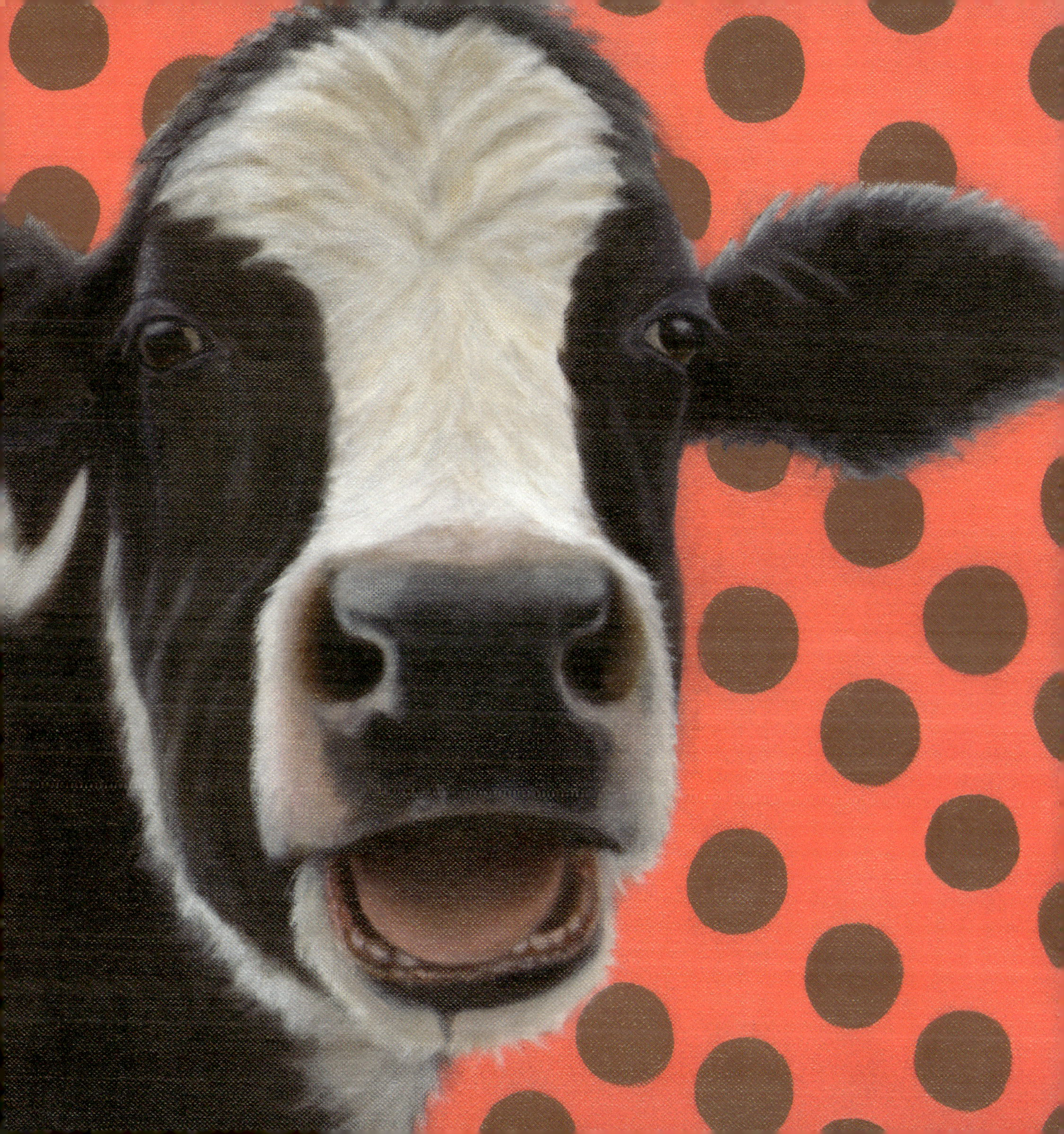

H2-Ooooh

Painted on blue
for a very good reason
I love to swim
no matter the season

Come along with me
let's take a quick dip
while you're paddling around
try a little sip

I know it is chilly
but water is my thing
would I look too silly
wearing water wings?

Get the towel ready
it's my most favorite part
when you wrap me and rub me
it sends waves through my heart

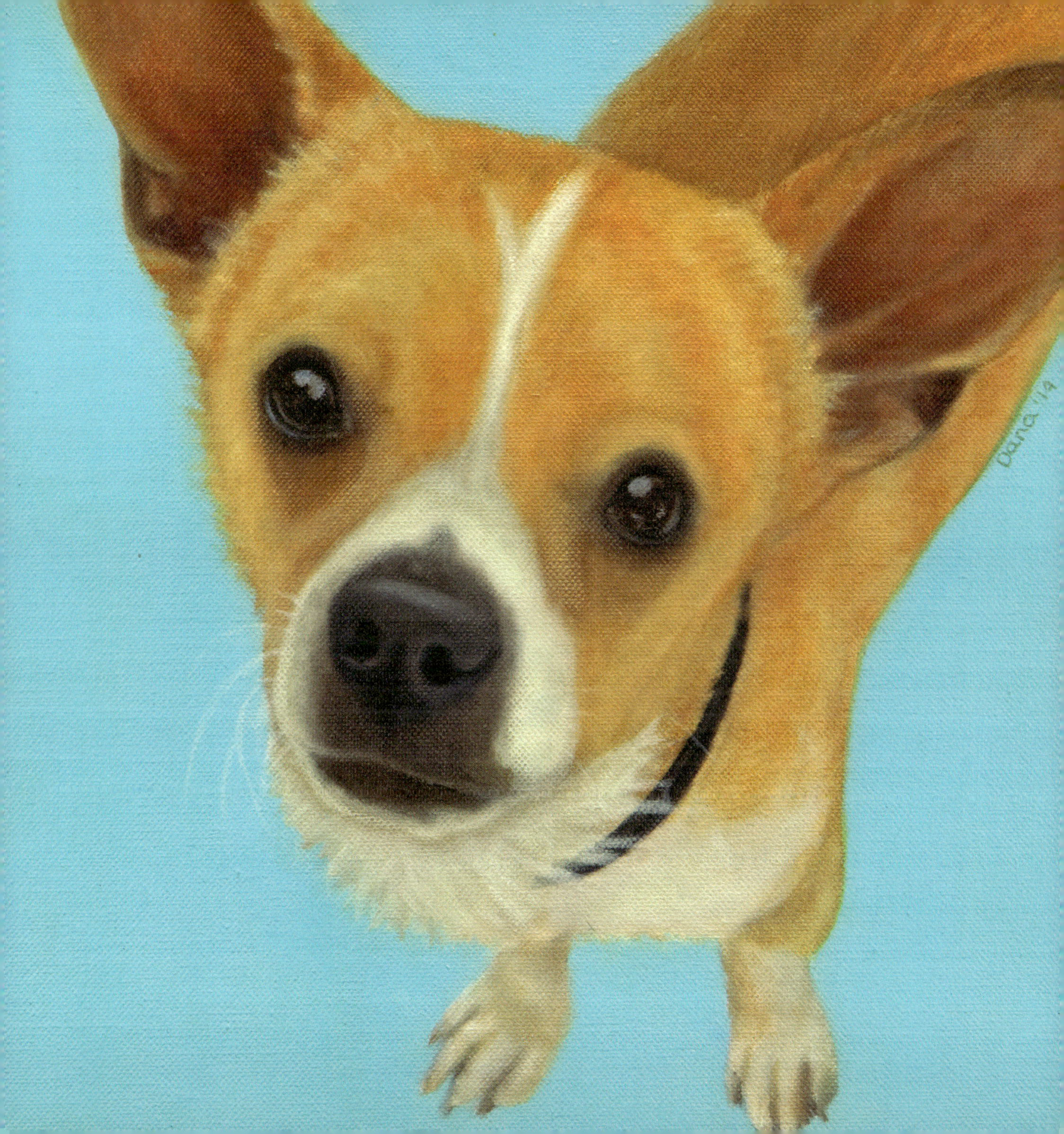

dots & daisy

look at these eyes
look at this nose
look at these adorable
spots on my toes

it's as good a time as any
to accept defeat

put your hand in the cookie jar
and give me a treat

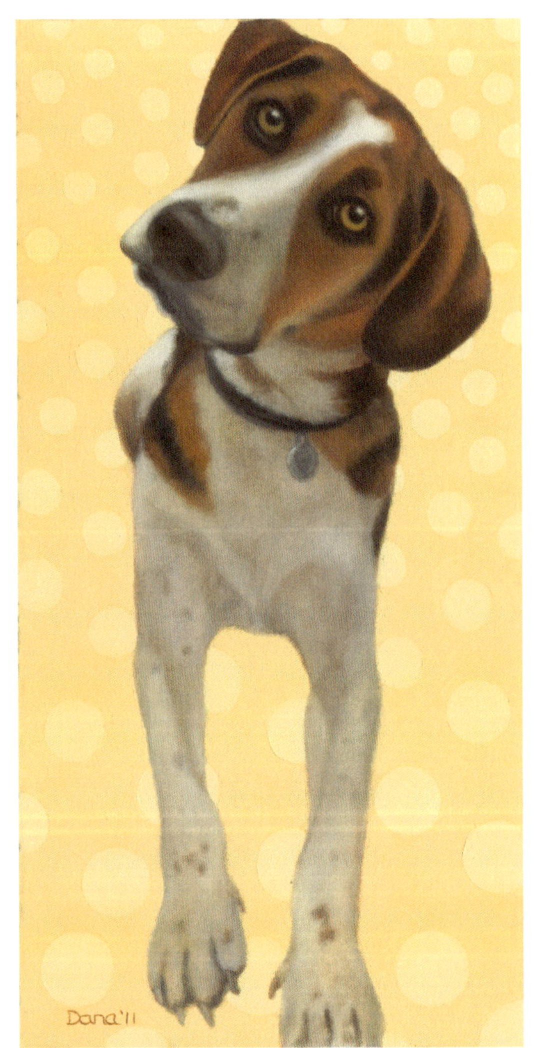

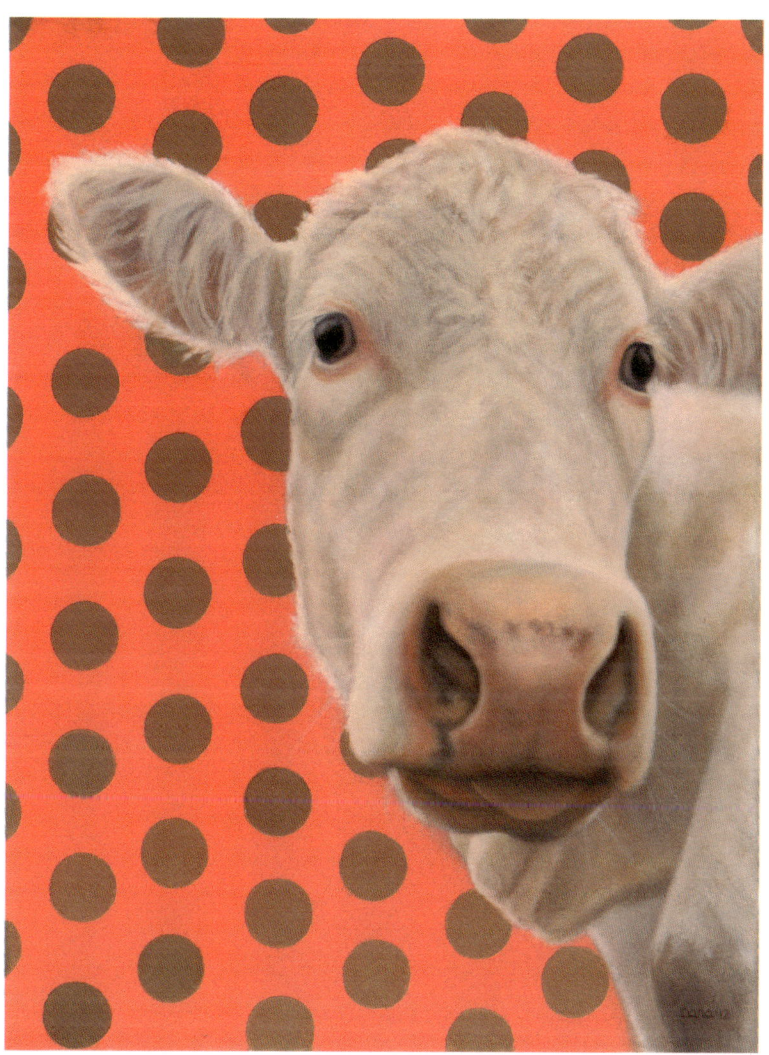

Who you be?

Be joy

Be compassion

Be love

Be kind

Be generous

Be listen

Be heard

Be quiet

Be still

Be free

Be happy

Be vegan

Be me

Beauty Is Only Feather Deep

What do you think
of my current 'do?
Is the color all right?
Or should I try something new?

As a rooster I struggle
with just the right coif.
Is it straight and centered,
or maybe a bit off?

It's not just my ego;
my hair is my story.
In fact, my dear friends,
it is my crowning glory.

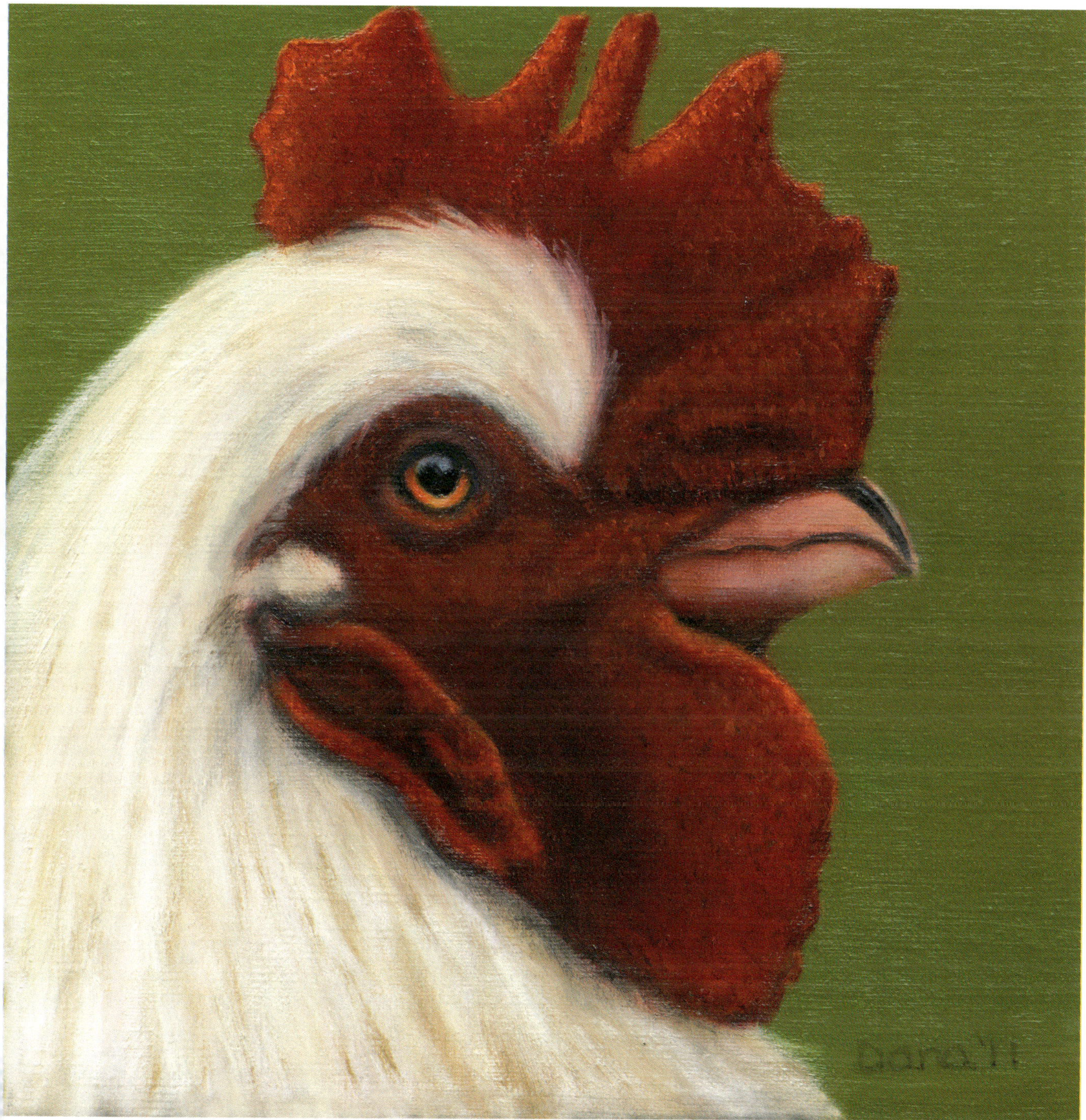

Short Order

I am a wee dog
so low to the ground
my toes small and soft
hardly make a sound

I like it down here
but it sure would be sweet
if every now and then
you would de-stink your feet

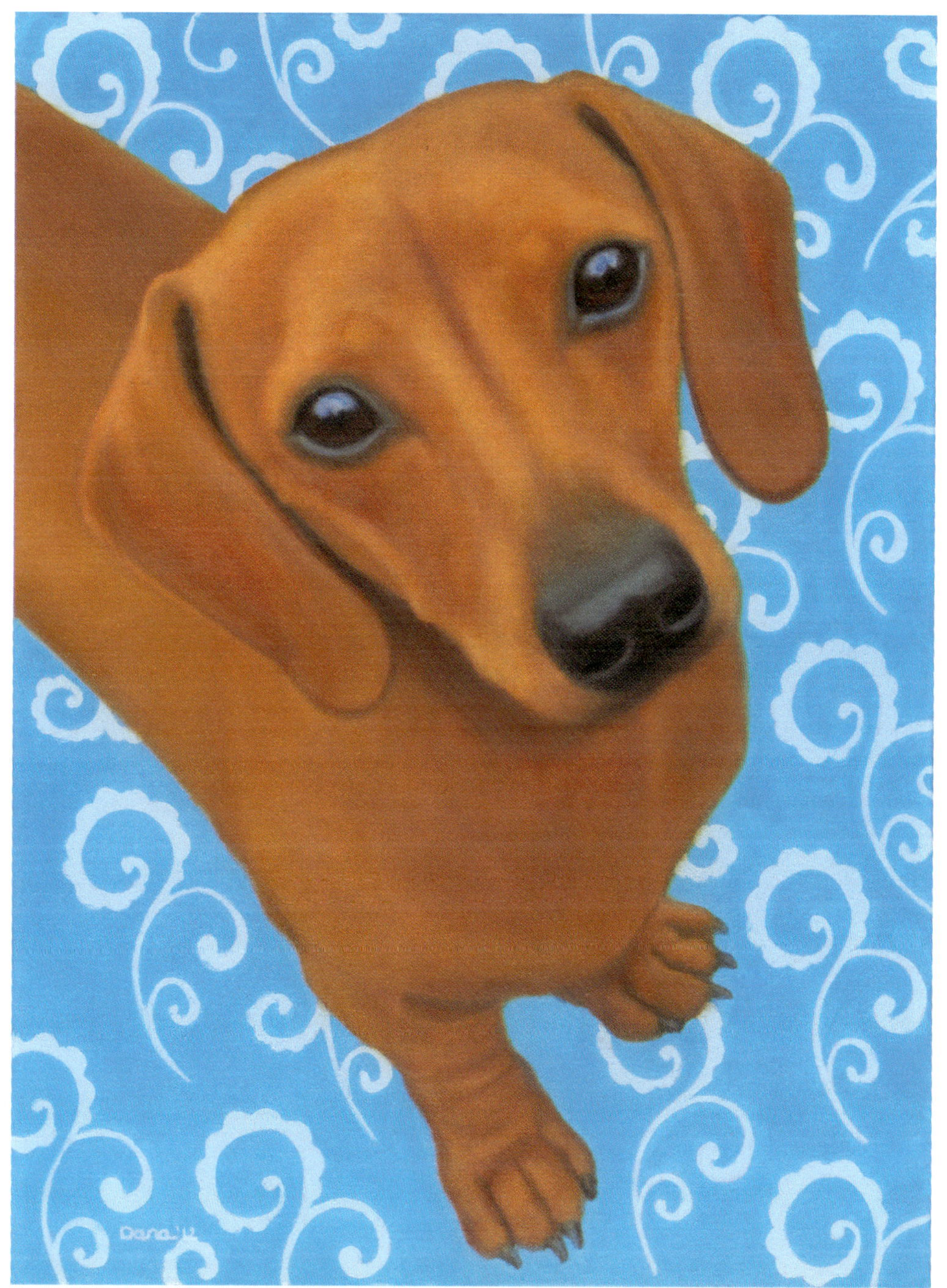

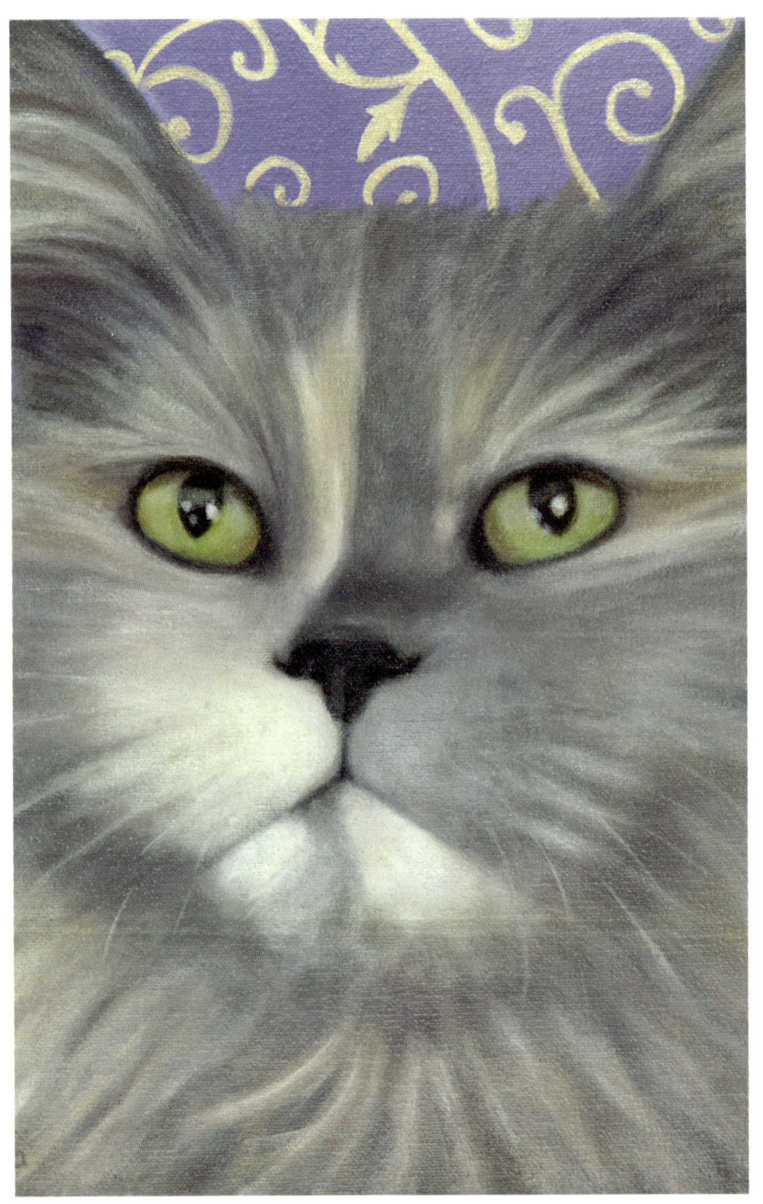

Home

life in the shelter
feels so helter-skelter
so many just like me
that I become hard to see

you pointed my way
and the cage was unlocked
you hugged me awhile
and we had a nice talk

when you put me back in
I began to cry
please oh please
don't tell me good-bye

fast forward a bit
I am brimming with love
in your home, on your lap
I comfortably sit

Equine Demure

She showed up last week
with a camera in hand
made me feel pretty
so chic, so grand

At first I was shy
felt a little out of place
because the artist's intent
was to paint my sweet face

I am no show pony
I am a rescue you see
don't want to appear phony
in any pictures of me

Now I hang on this wall
for all to admire
so regal, so tall
full of hope to inspire

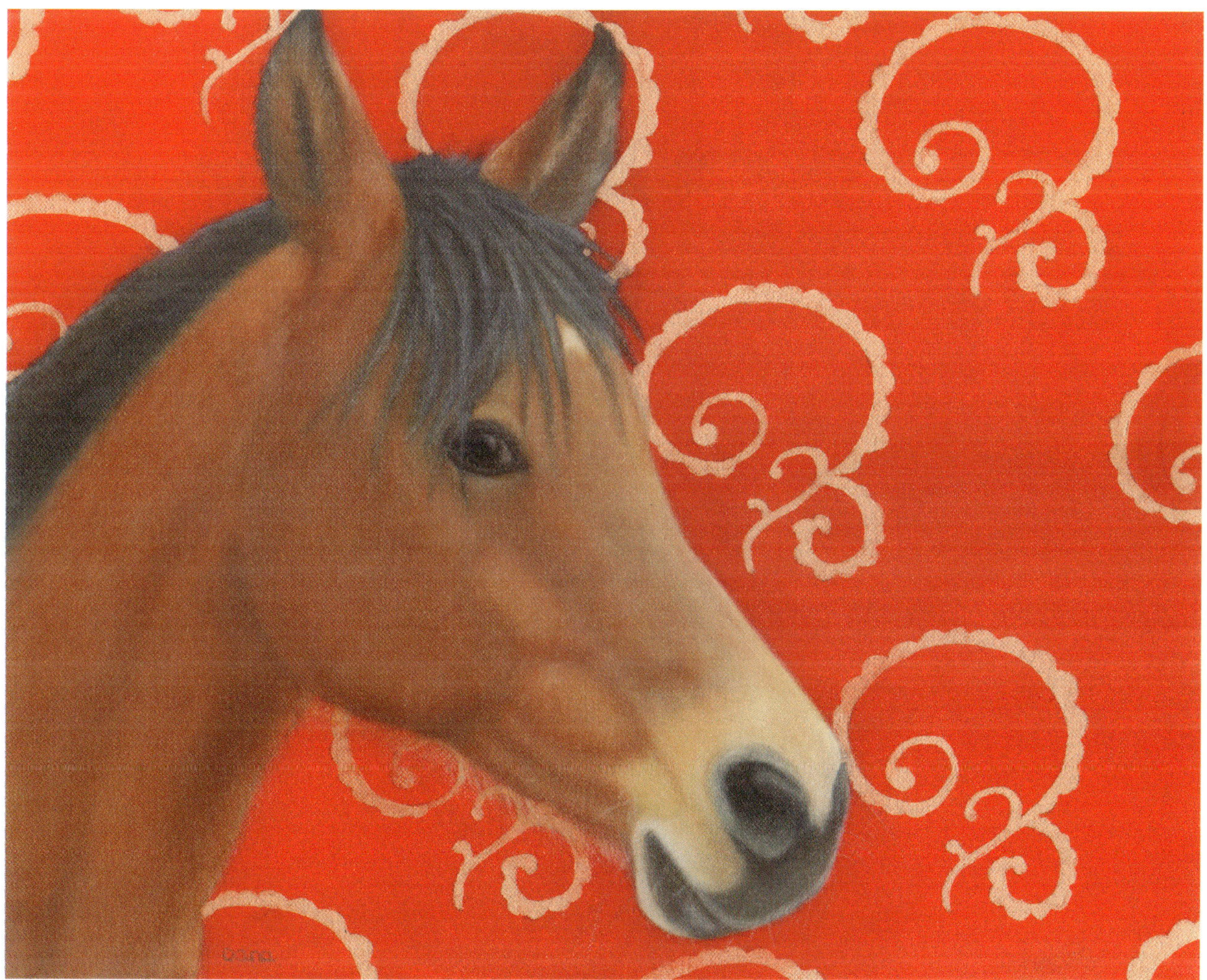

Three Amigos

Clifford and Roy
my two favorite boys
were rescued with me
how grateful are we!

Scooped up by heroes
who felt in their hearts
that our final fate
should not be served on a plate

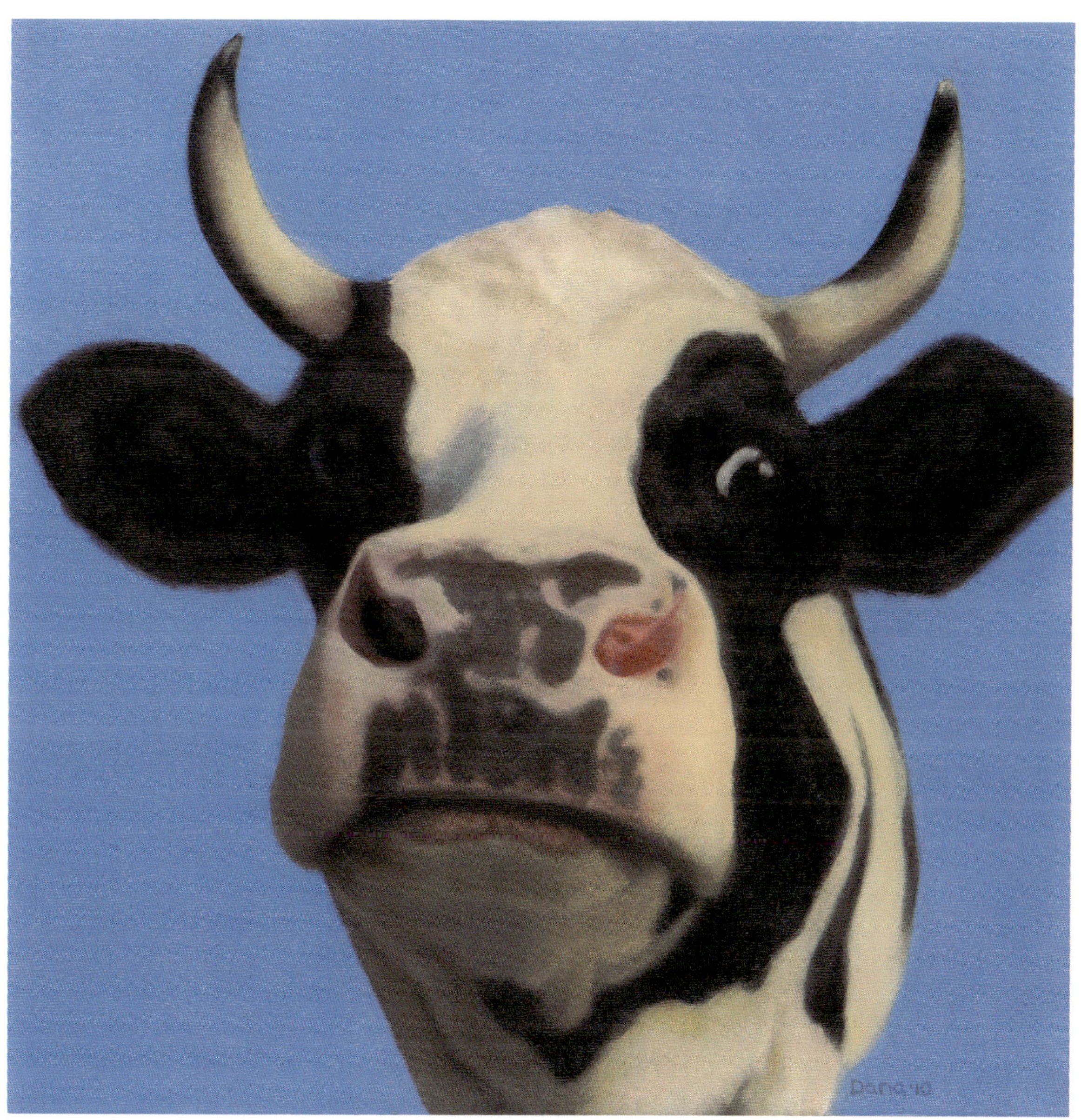

Never Hurts to Ask

Young Ellie thought
it was worth a phone call
to request that the artist
paint her kitty Snowball

Please paint my cat
the little girl said
no need for her body
it can just be her head

I love her so much
she is my best pal
if you paint her for me
she becomes immortal

An argument so sweet
the artist could not decline
so she painted a portrait
of Ellie's beautiful feline

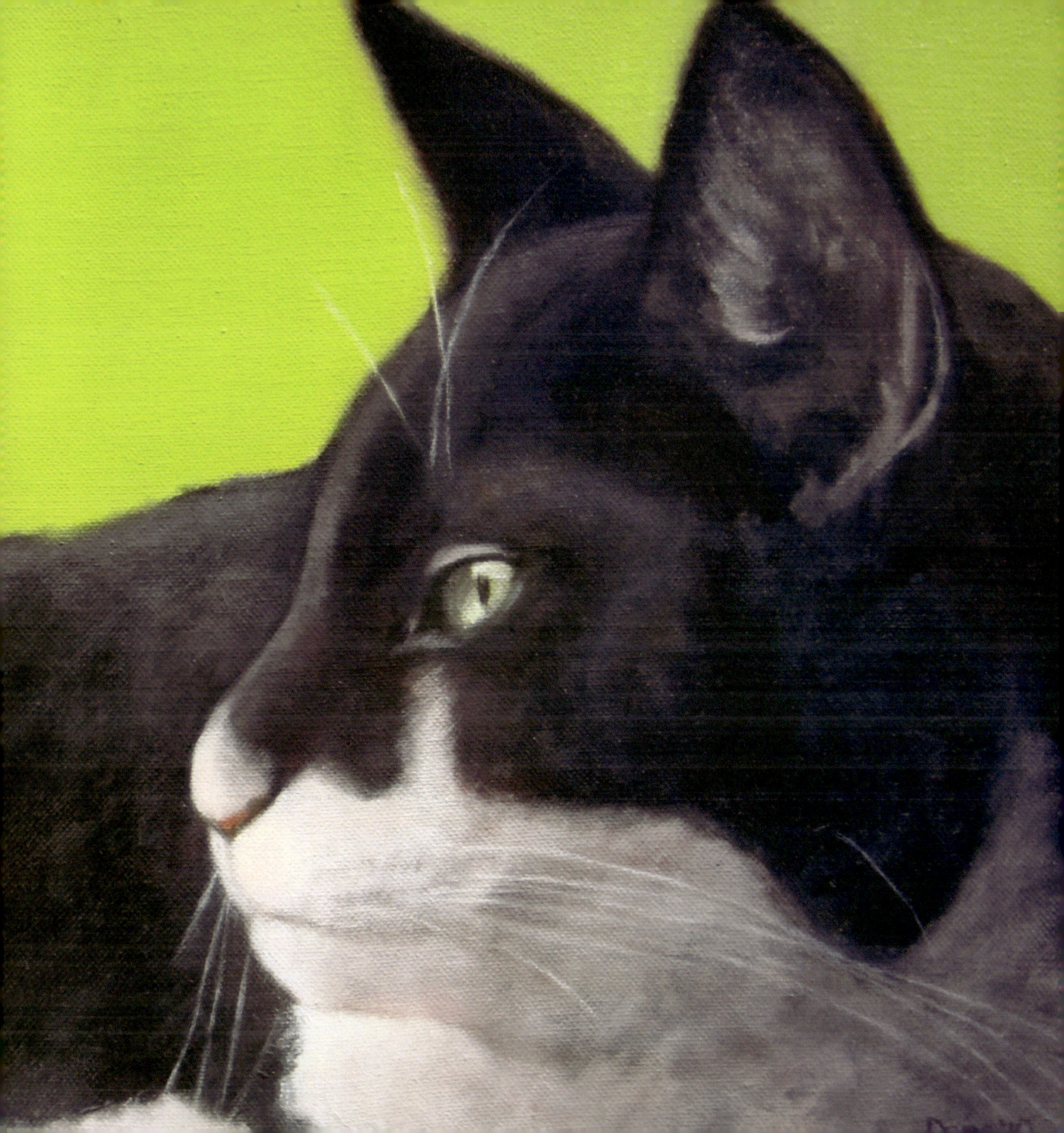

Artist's Muse

the kindness of humans
gave me a chance
to be cared for and loved
from only one glance

from a cage in the shelter
our eyes first met
a moment I am certain
neither will forget

she wanted a bunny
for most of her years
she heard my eyes saying
"here! I'm right here!"

I lived out my life
as her studio muse
the coziest place ever
with the best garden view

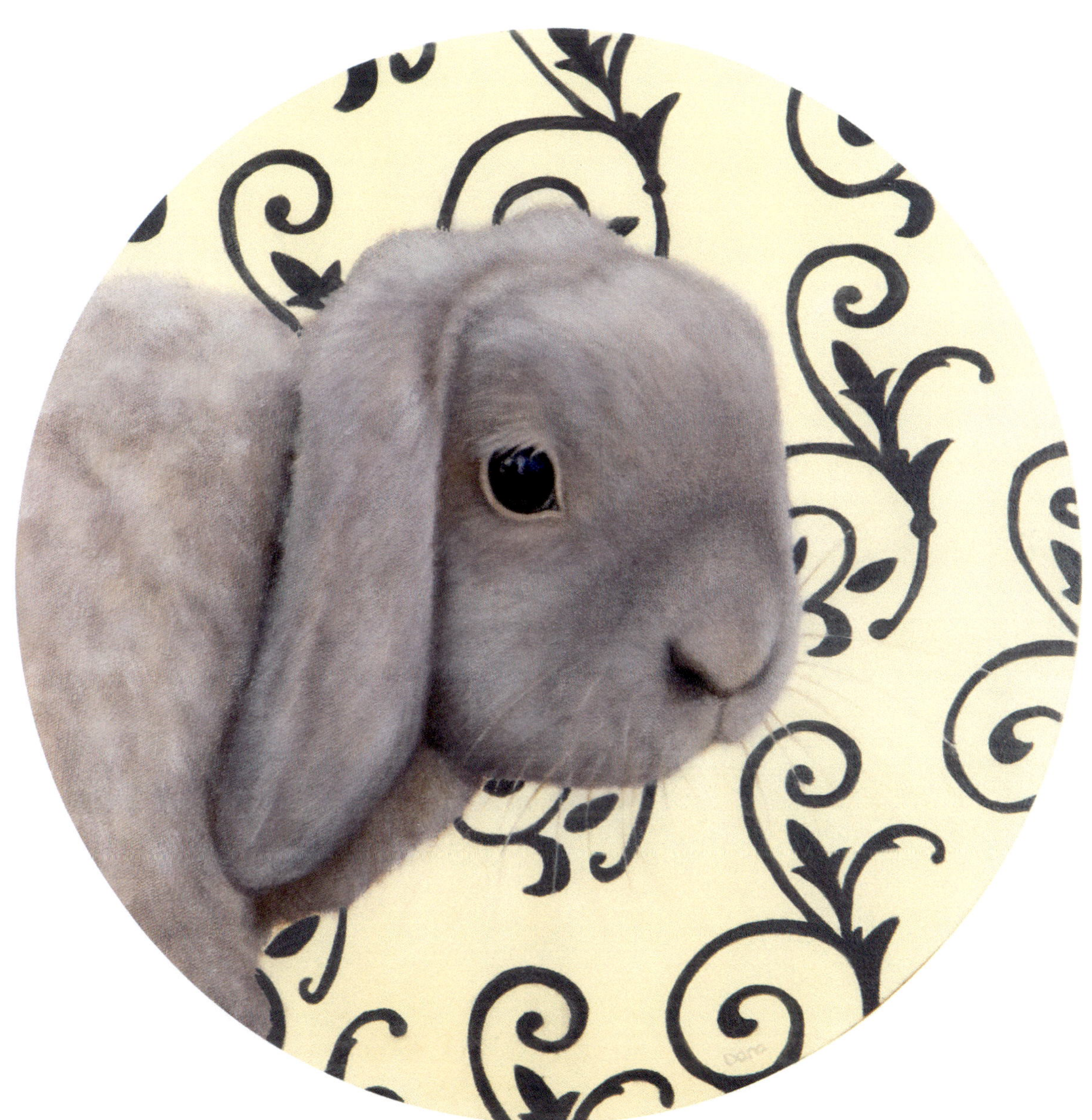

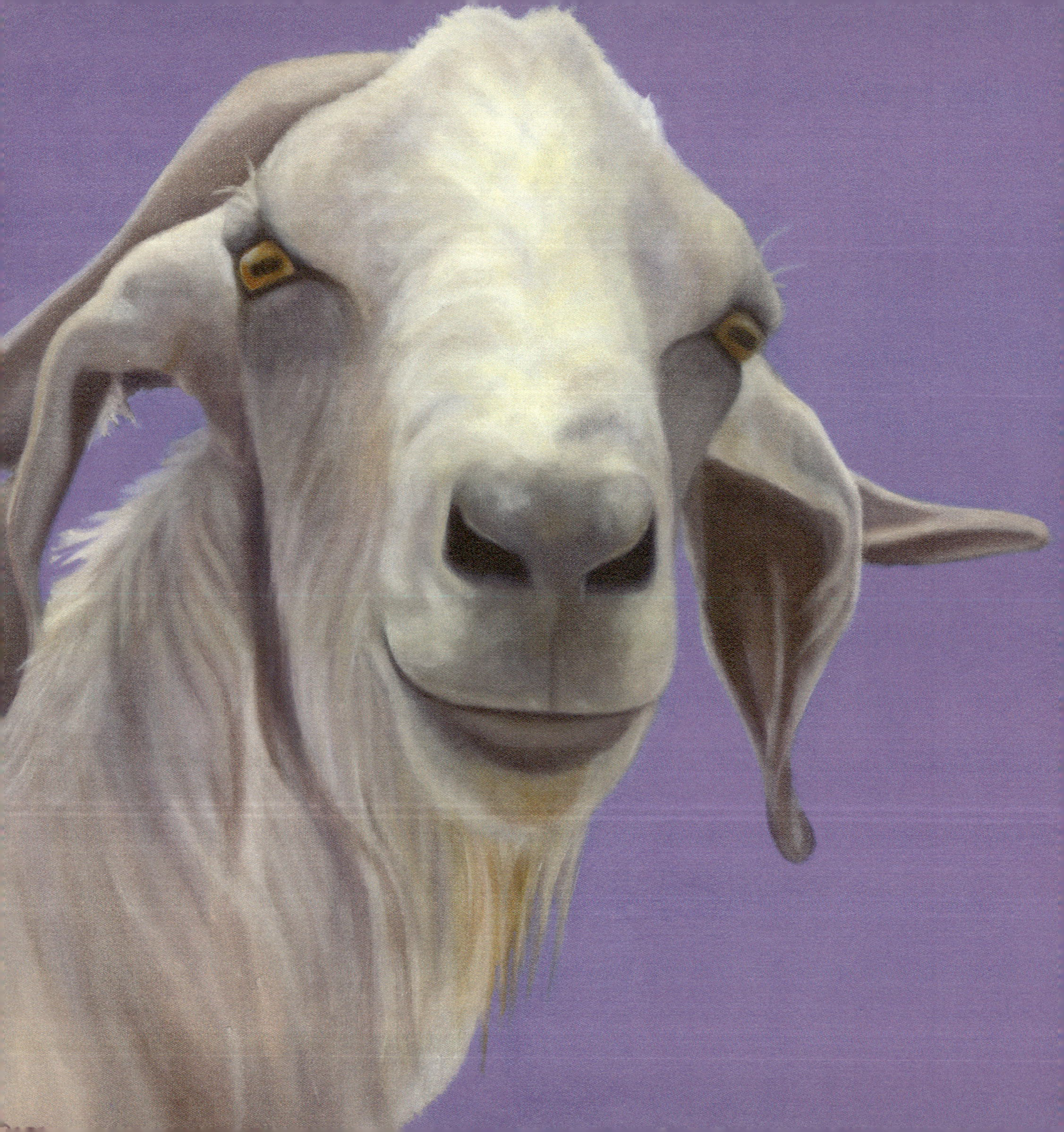

The Sweet Spot

I am a goat
and I had you at bleat
my horizontal eyes
and my sweet cloven feet

I will be your best friend
if you scratch between my horns
yes! that is the spot
where it is completely unworn

delivered to you
by the Universe's grace
if I call you my bestie
will you scratch my whole face?

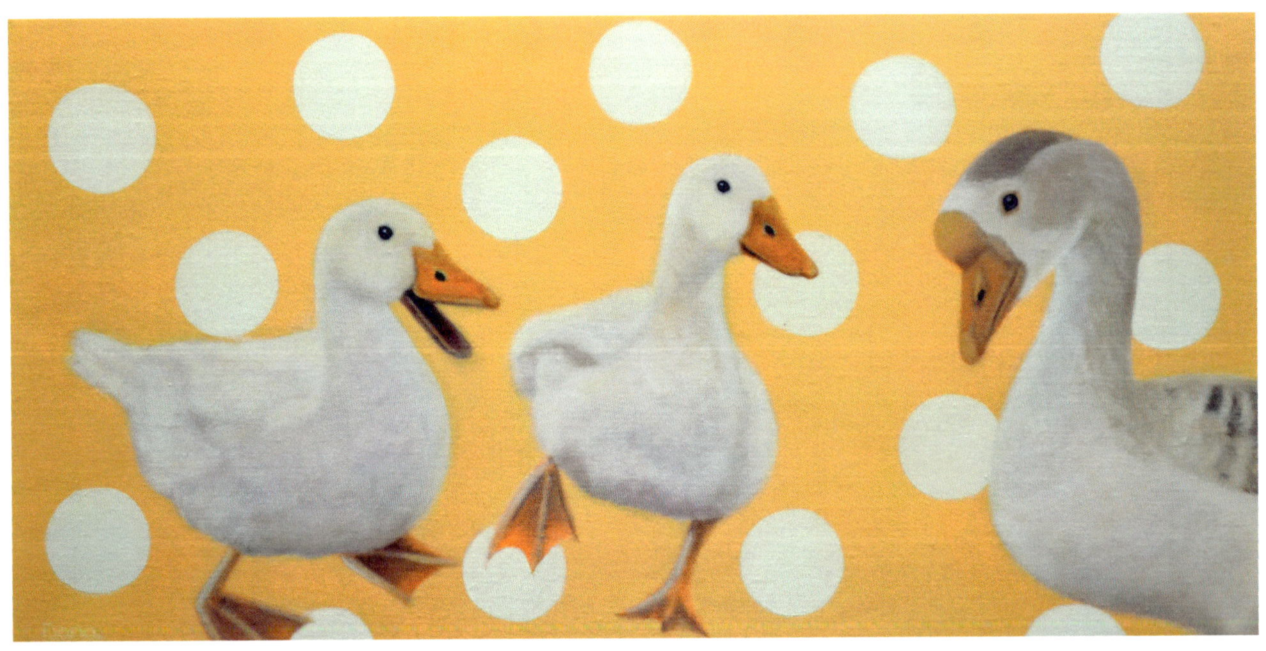

Duck, Duck, GOOSE

You know the game
you have played it before
we have a new way
the old way's a bore

Instead of a circle
we like a straight line
and our favorite new rule
is you must always drink wine

When you tap my beak
and say the word GOOSE
you must waddle a straight line
or risk getting a deuce

It doesn't much matter
how tipsy we get
we do not drive cars
so you need not fret

Hidden Agenda

I do things in secret
every movement covert
each bone that I bury
well covered with dirt

You think I am sleeping
but I am awake
with one eye barely open
there is too much at stake

don't let this face fool you
my cuteness a mask
question my motives
and I will take you to task

I keep my agenda
close to the cuff
not completely hidden
but it's close enough

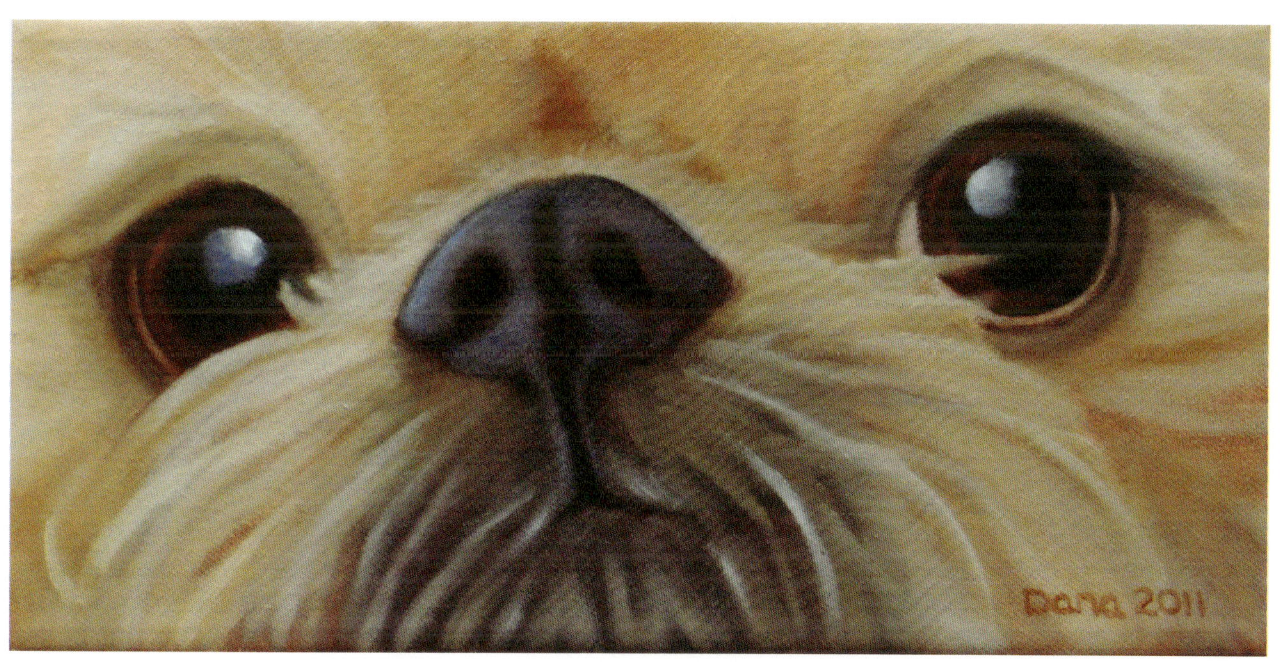

Heck with eHarmony

I am a shy little goose,
trying hard to cut loose,
to find a suitable date
without tempting fate.

I've tried Match and Tinder,
but both only hinder
my ability to be
the real true me.

Bars are too sinistery,
Christian Mingle too ministery,
and speed dating too quick
for me to properly pick.

There is one more choice
to find true love's voice.
If I am done being lonely
I must try Farmers Only.

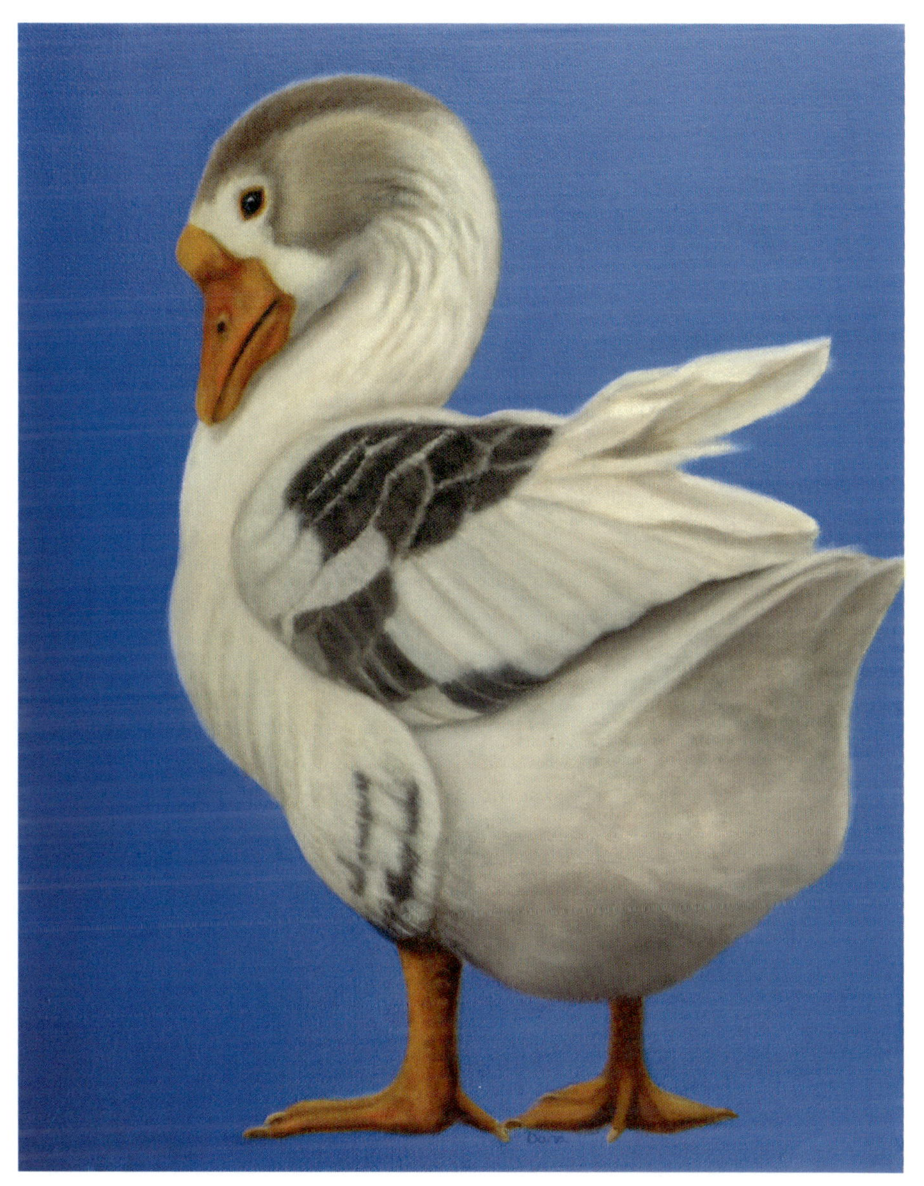

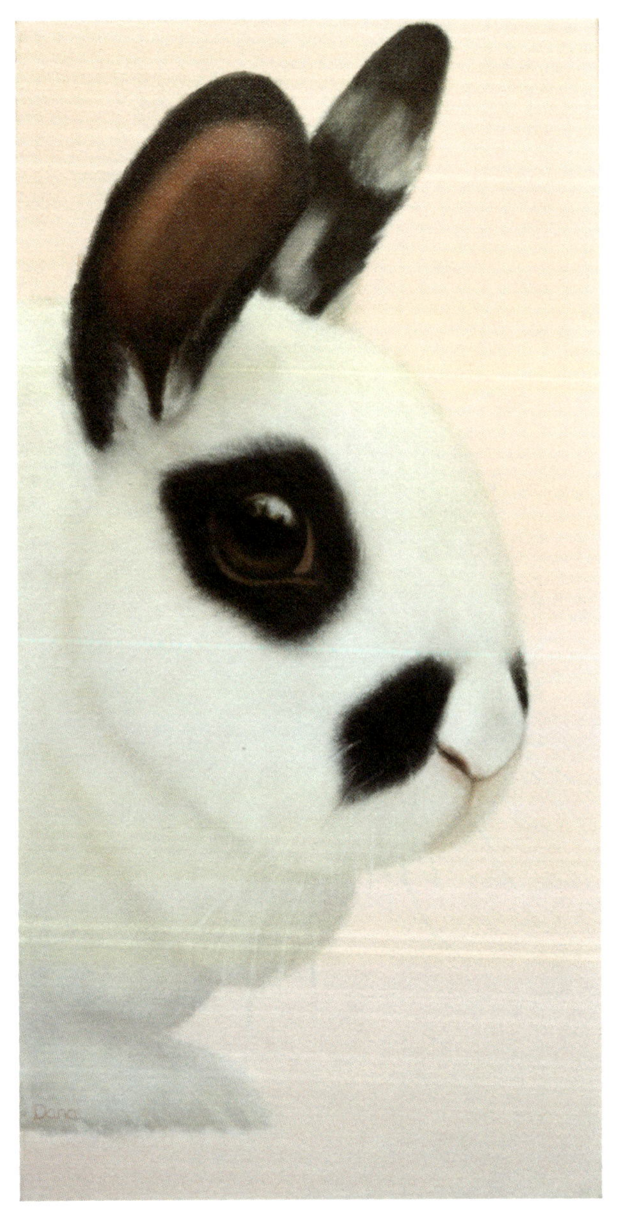

60

Go Stew Yourself

I am not a collar
or a good-luck charm.
Why would anyone want
to cause me such harm?

Your jackets can be made
of fur that is faux;
your makeup can be tested
on the nonliving, you know?

We bunnies we feel
both fear and pain.
Eating us for dinner
is completely insane!

For vitamins and protein
there are other means.
Try eating what I eat:
yummy carrots and greens.

Résumé

My name is Riley
I come recommended highly
I am a chaser of balls
stellar references, go ahead, call

My skills are so great
none else need apply
never drop it halfway
or stop for a pee

All bosses love me
just ask them, it's true
because when you throw a ball
I always bring it back to you

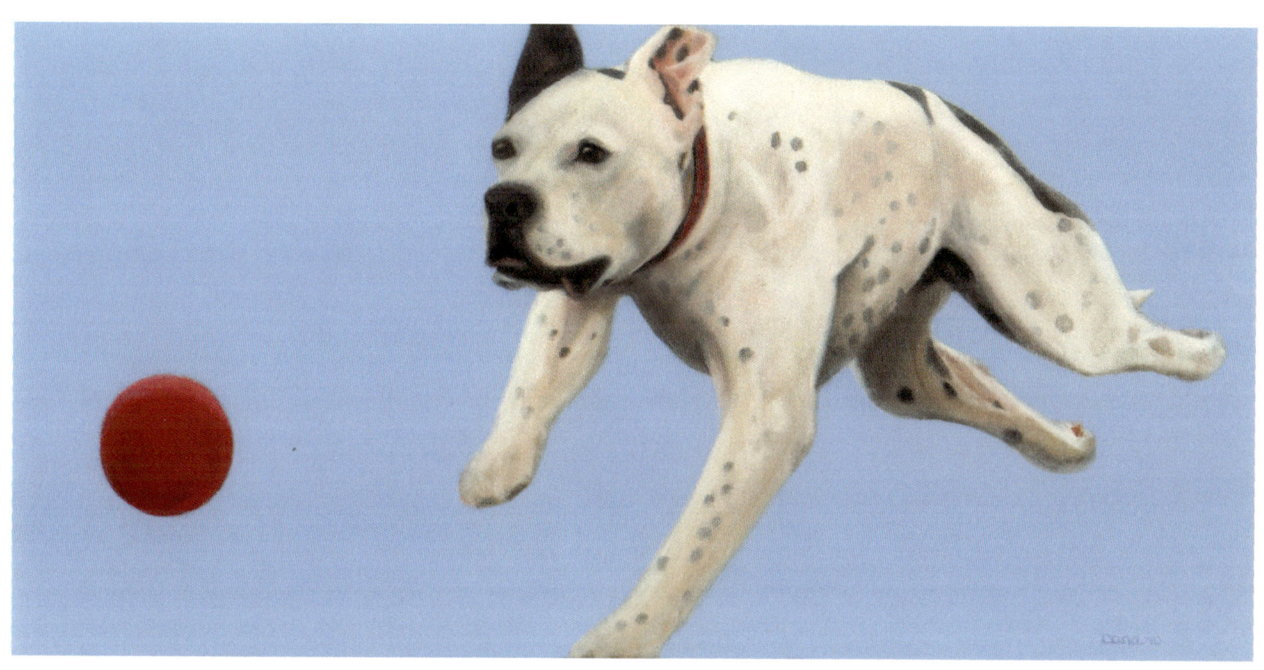

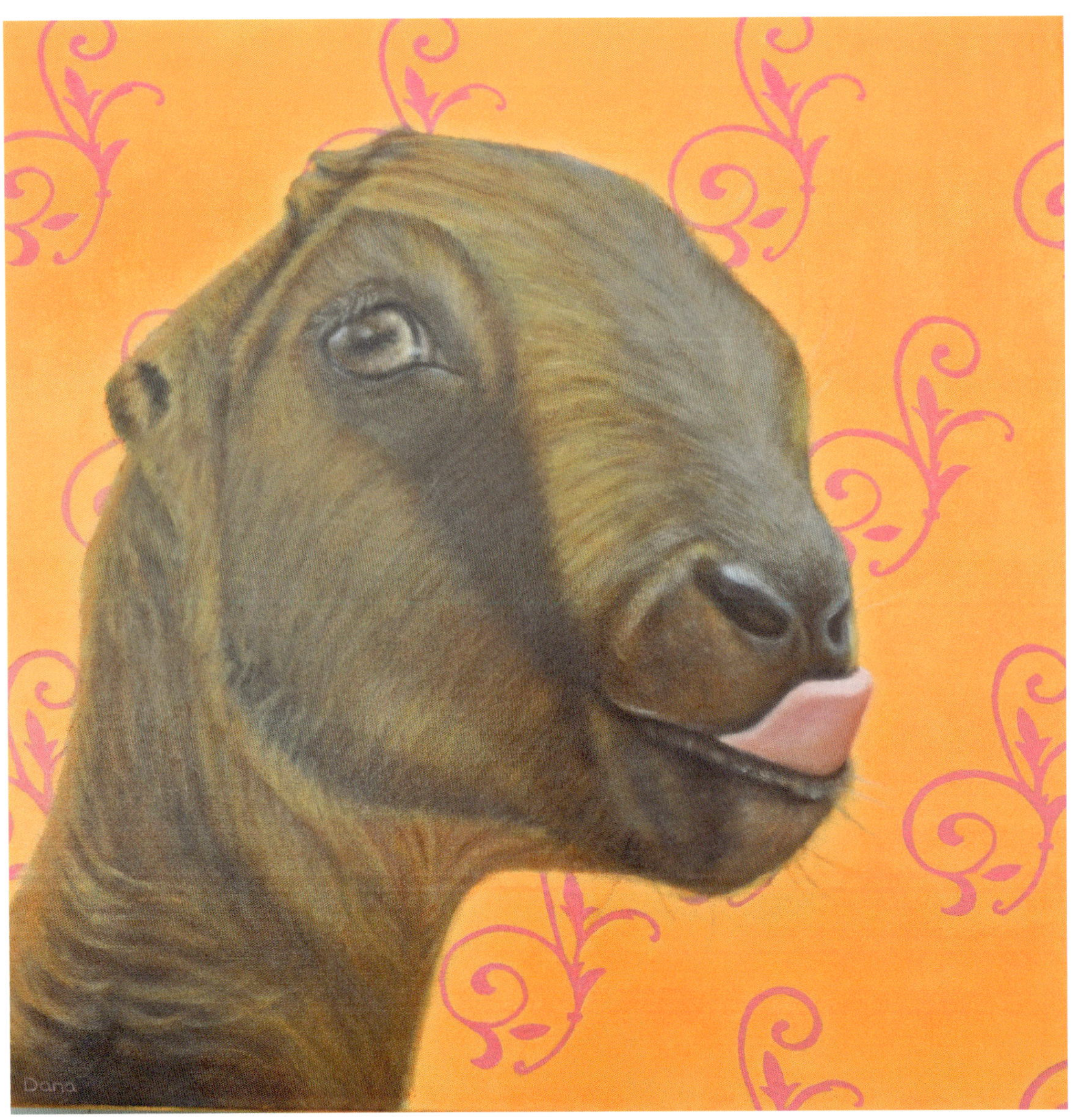

Dana

Hear this!

Don Quixote
had nothing to do
with bringing me here
do you know who?

Her name was Eula
or Mrs. Fay Frey
she loved my rich milk
which people loved to buy

Bred from the start
on an Oregon knoll
my ears so sweet
like tiny cinnamon rolls

With Eula long gone
and so many other choices
LaManchas deserve
to have heard their voices

Go milk an almond
instead of our teats
eat yummy grilled soy burgers
but *never* grilled meats

Canine Service Announcement

I herald from greatness
it's right there in my name
enormous responsibility
accompanies my fame

I am spreading a message
to be gentle and kind
it's part of my contract
a purer heart's tough to find

I ask you to be cautious
when purchasing a breed
some breeders are scary
and breed only out of greed

Please check shelters and rescues
before writing that check
and save a sweet orphan
from a life of neglect

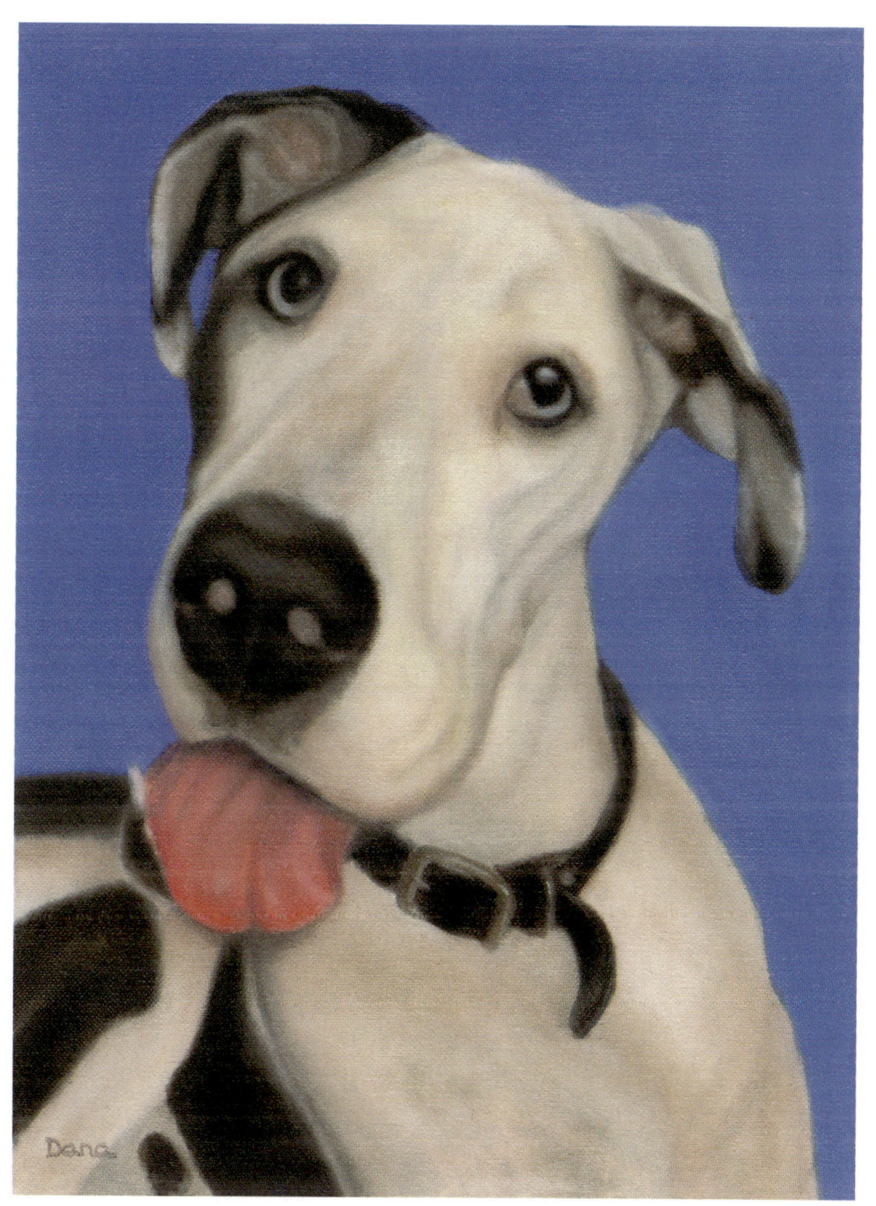

Ready for My Close-up

A horse might only
be a horse,
of course,
but what of a mare
who continues to stare
at her own reflection,
like a model of sorts
who eats hay
and snorts
and likes having a mirror
so she can see clearer
what a beauty she is
so pretty
in fact
she should be
in show biz

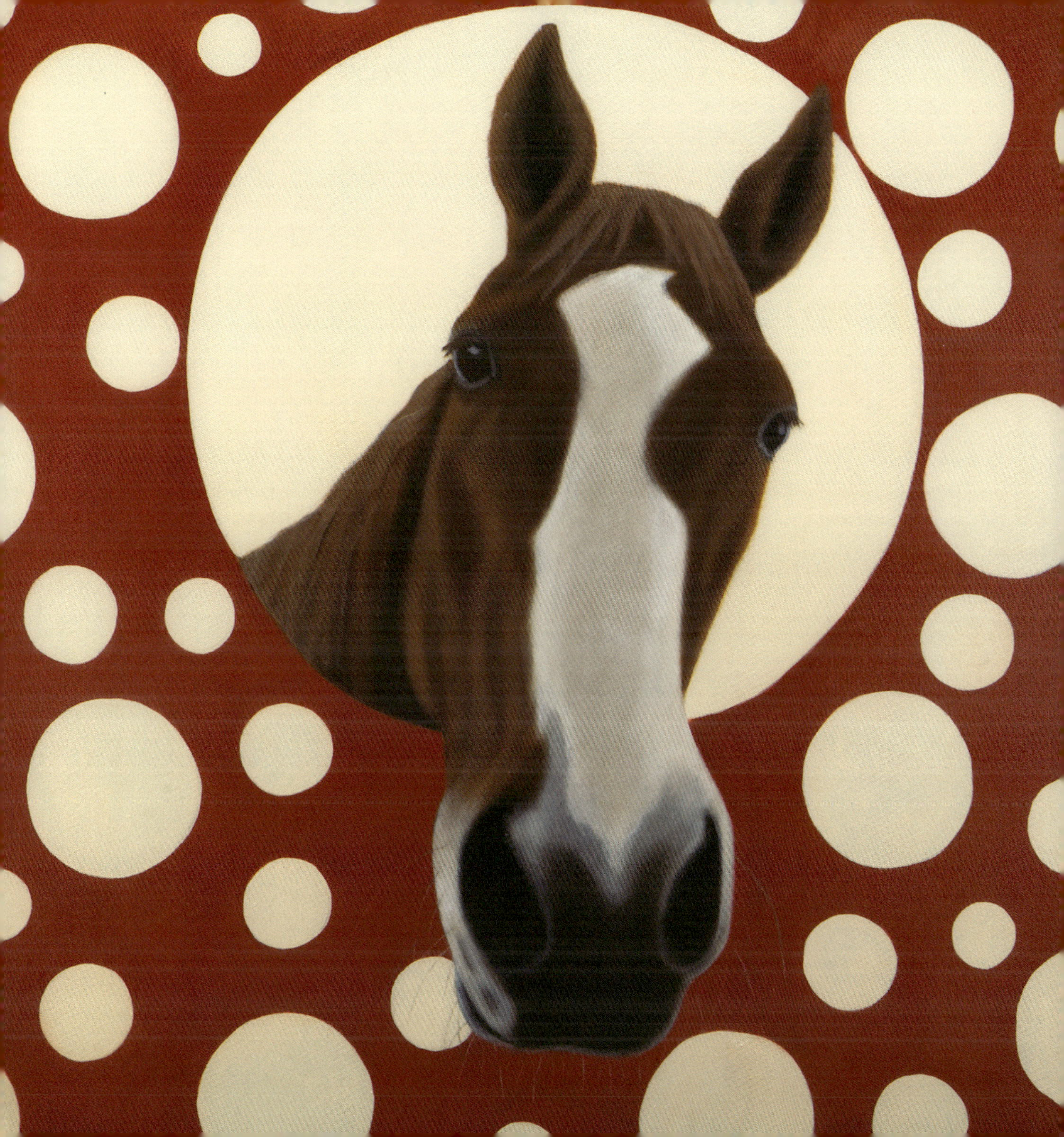

Delicious Donkey Ears

Inside
outside
along the side
around the side
Not a race
Slow it down
Take your time
Rub every inch
of my delicious
donkey ears

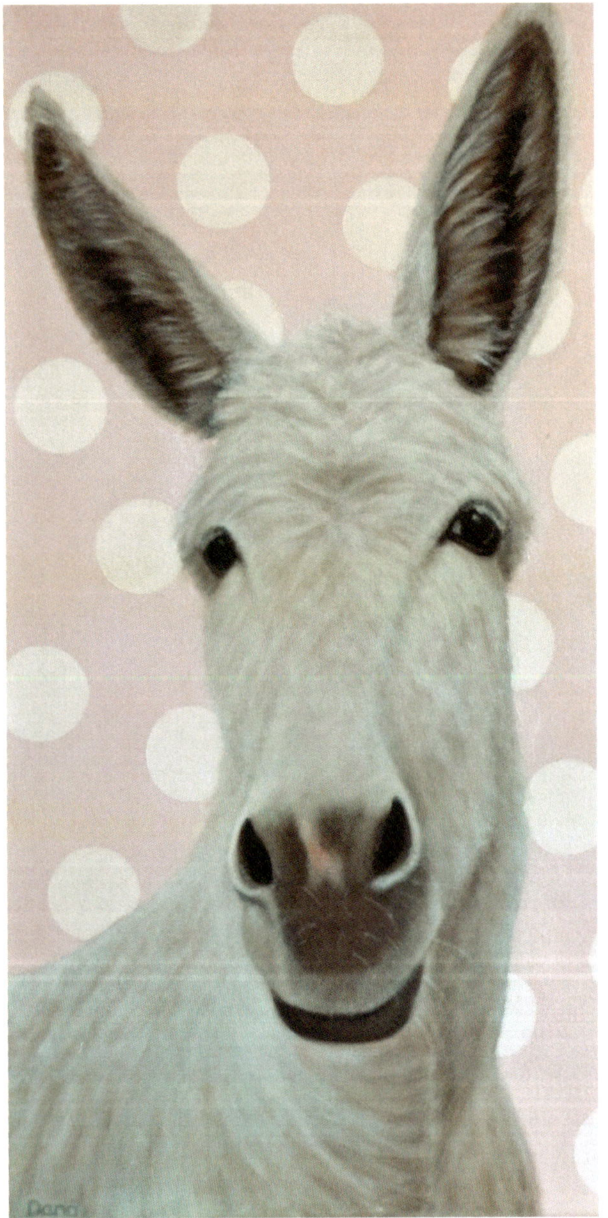

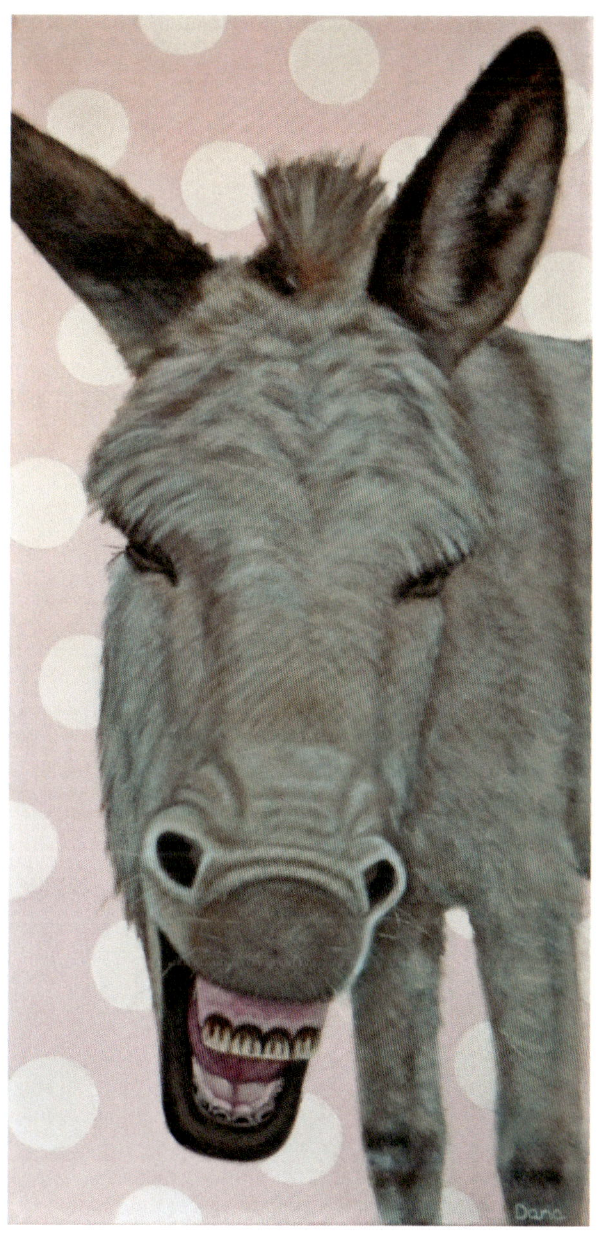

Don't You Carrot All?

It's true I am small,
but not quite a mini.

Not a black Jack,
but a silvery Jenny.

I flutter my lashes
and sing you a song;
it sounds more like a squeak
and isn't very long.

Nonetheless my ode
is a polite request
for that delicious crisp orange treat
that grows in the ground.

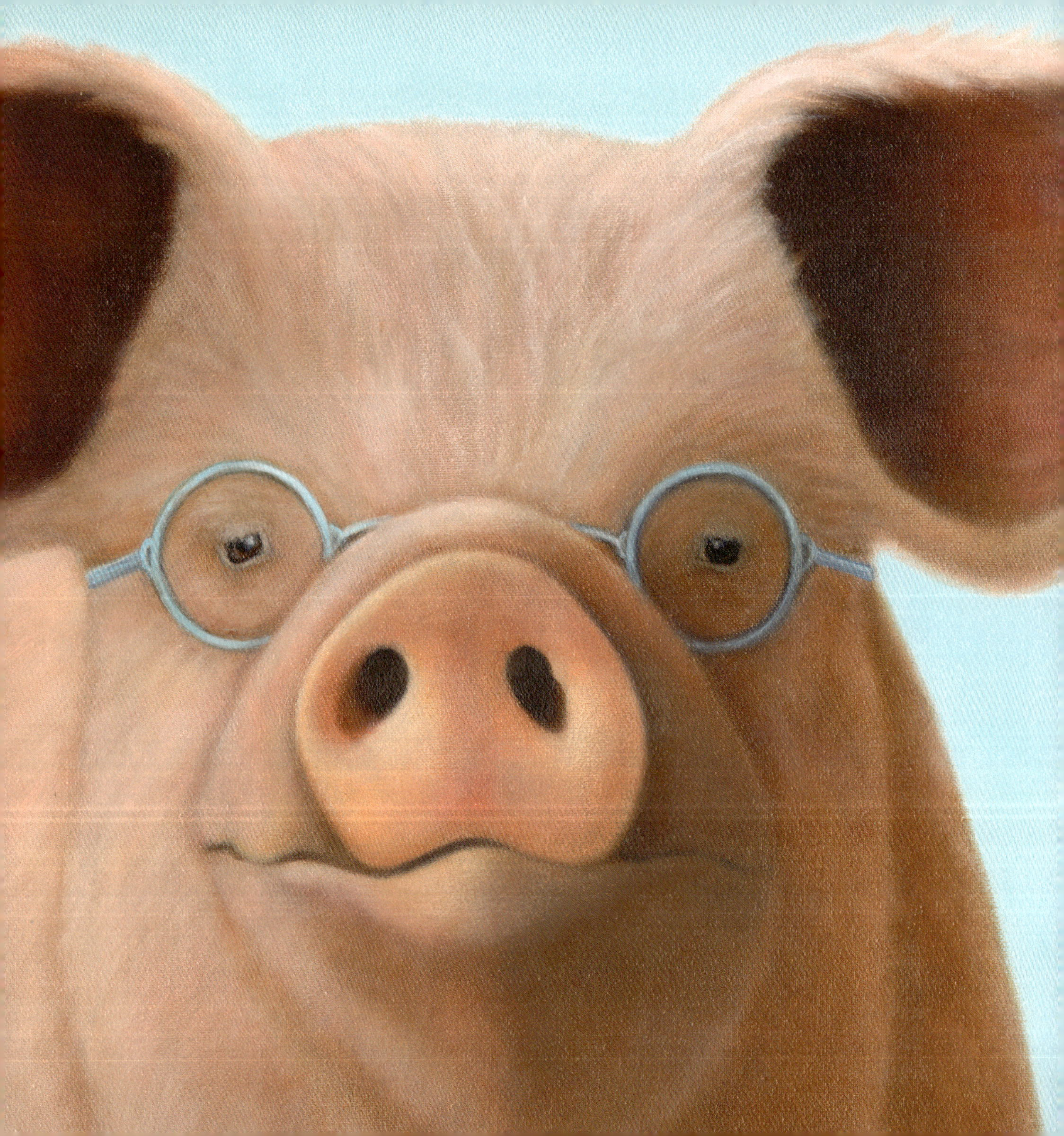

The Whole Package

My virtues are great,
as all porcine are.

Had I thumbs that were opposable,
I could drive your nice car.

My intelligence is remarkable;
cats & dogs it surpasses.

IQ scores aside,
this question, it burns—

Do sows still make passes
at pigs who wear glasses?

Change Is Good

The sky is blue,
but not my mood.
I was rescued today,
and will not be your food.

No more days at the factory;
those machines were so scary.
Humans are so silly;
there is no reason for dairy.

There are soy beans and nuts
and plants from the ground
that make yummy milk and cheeses;
such choices abound.

It makes such good sense
and it's easy to see
you should eat what I eat,
instead of eating me.

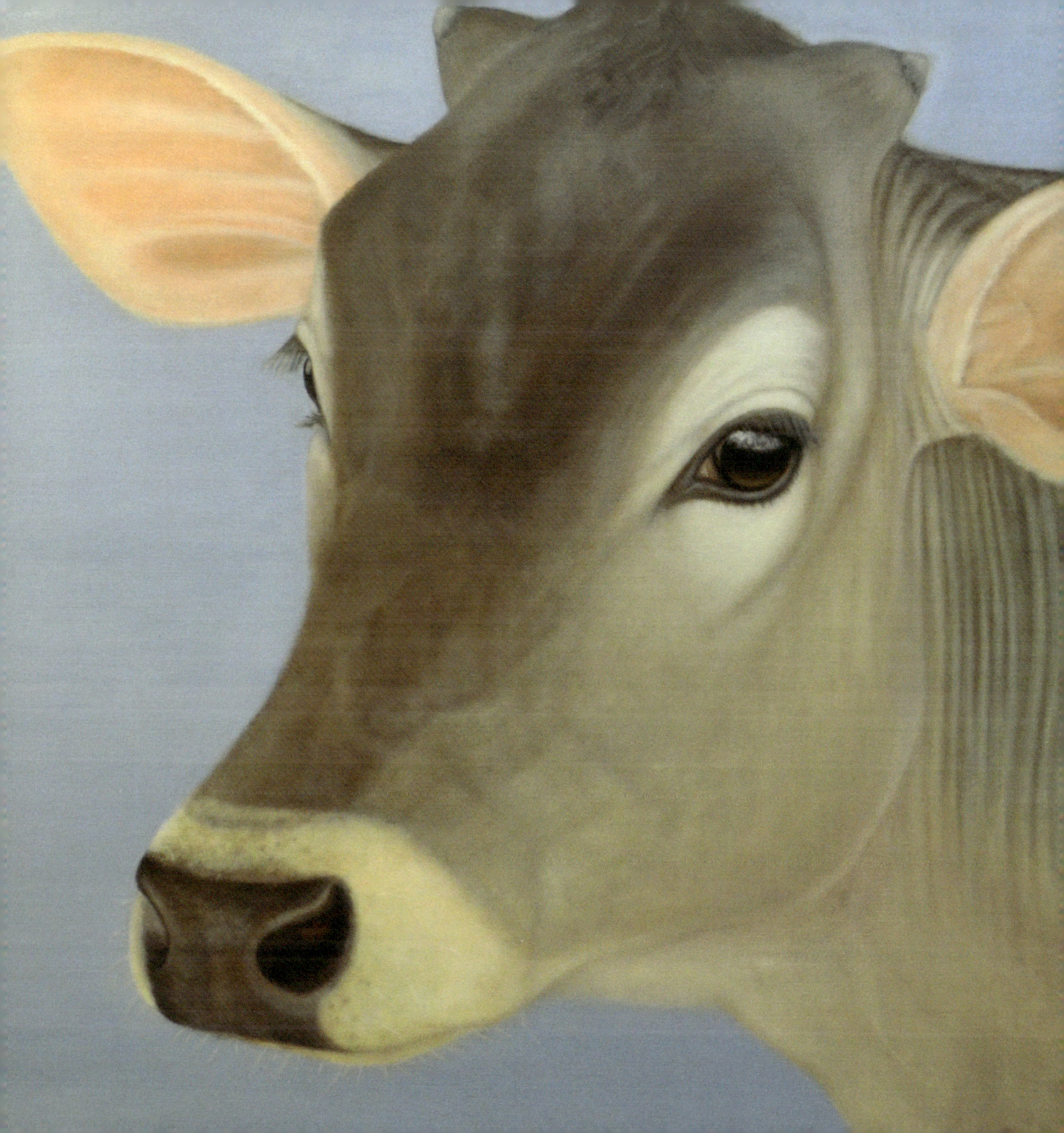

Division of
Dog & State

King Charles and son
both adored my sweet mug
but my reign ended there
because of the pug

When the House of Stuart fell
the Tudors felt compelled
to name my breed treason
for some ridiculous reason

But I found my way back
in spite of those thugs
and I am proud to report
some of my best friends are pugs

Pardon me if I sound cavalier
but a breed has no bearing
on appearance or smarts
true import lies in the size of one's heart

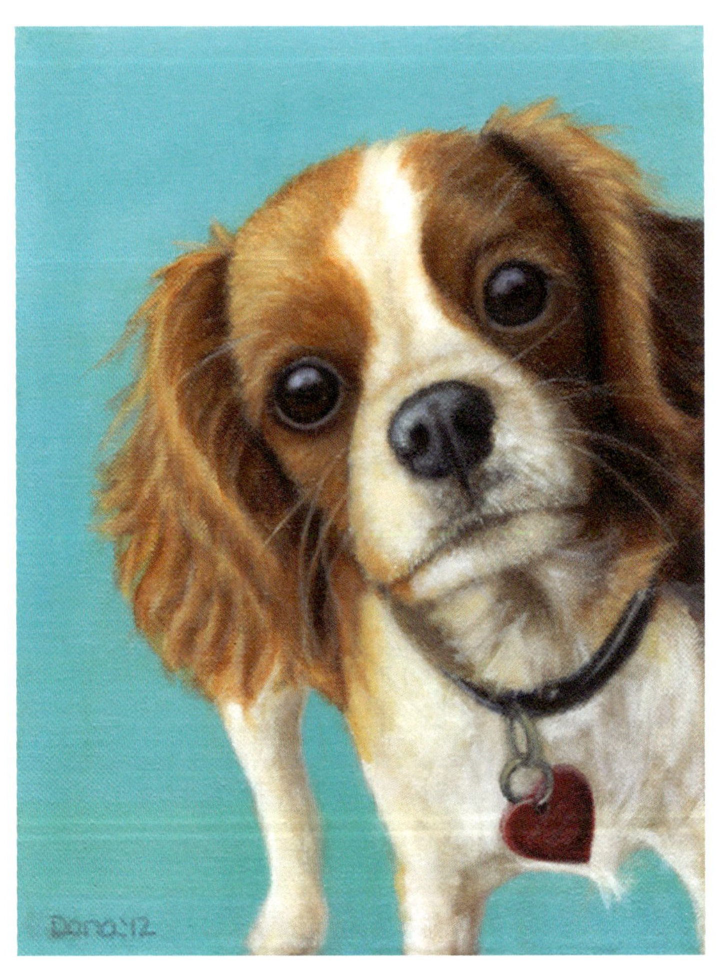

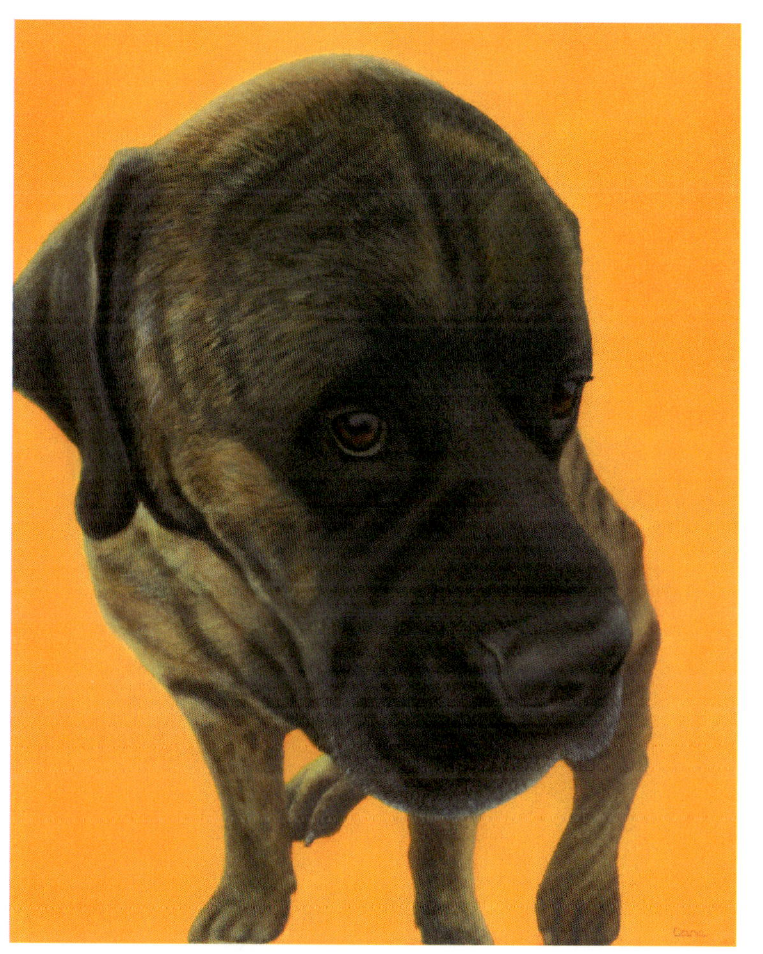

It Wasn't Me

If I avert my eyes
then you cannot tell
that the slipper you are missing
just gained admission to hell

It tasted great
as it met its sad fate
I left you the other one
but I am not yet quite done

I know I'm in trouble
but please don't be hasty
it's not really my fault
that your footwear is so tasty

Made You Look

I took a peek
and what did I find?
That my pretty new home
is one of a kind.

I share a large pond
with several geese;
they hail from Canada
and always come in peace.

For bringing me here,
I am grateful, you know,
'cause otherwise I might hang
in a storefront window.

You probably just winced
as you read that last line
so do something about it;
go vegan! It's time.

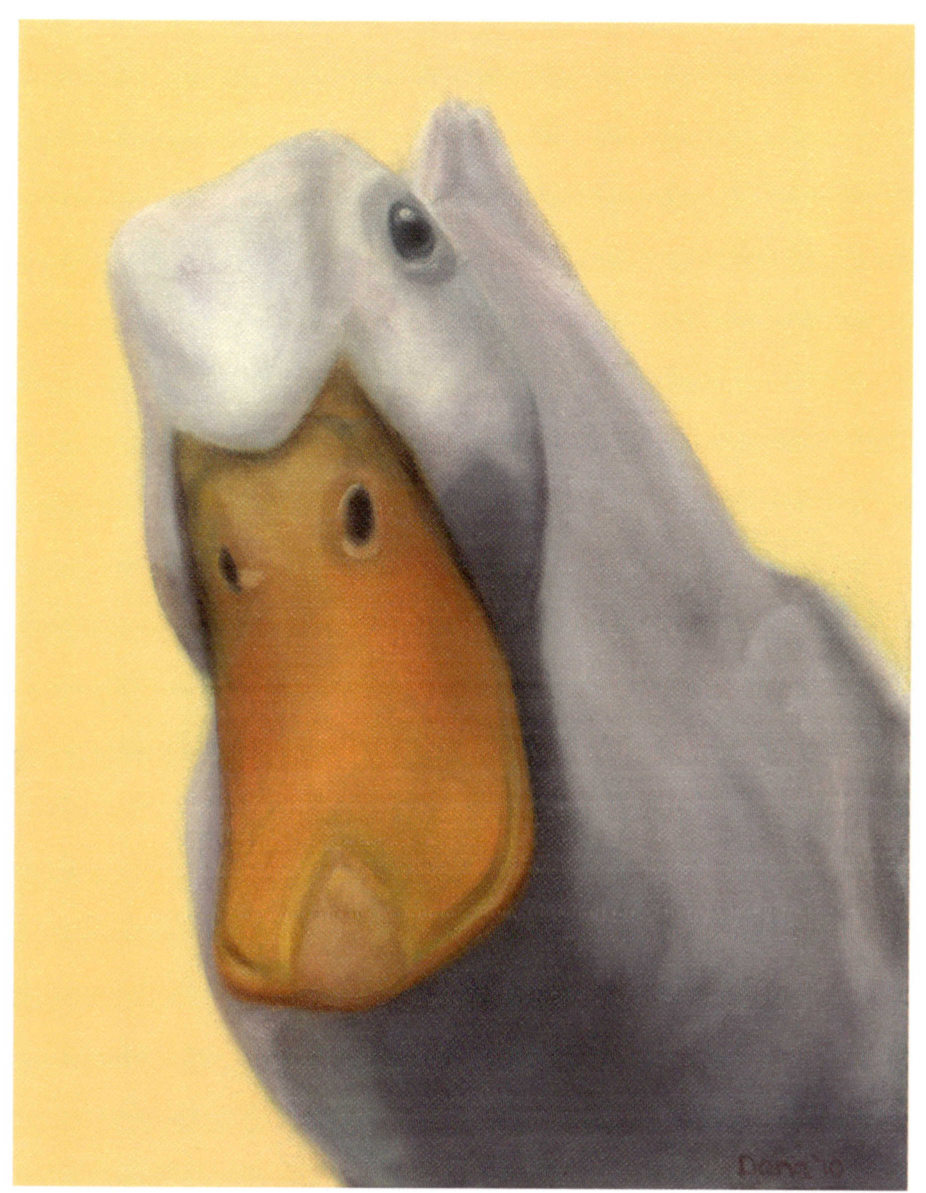

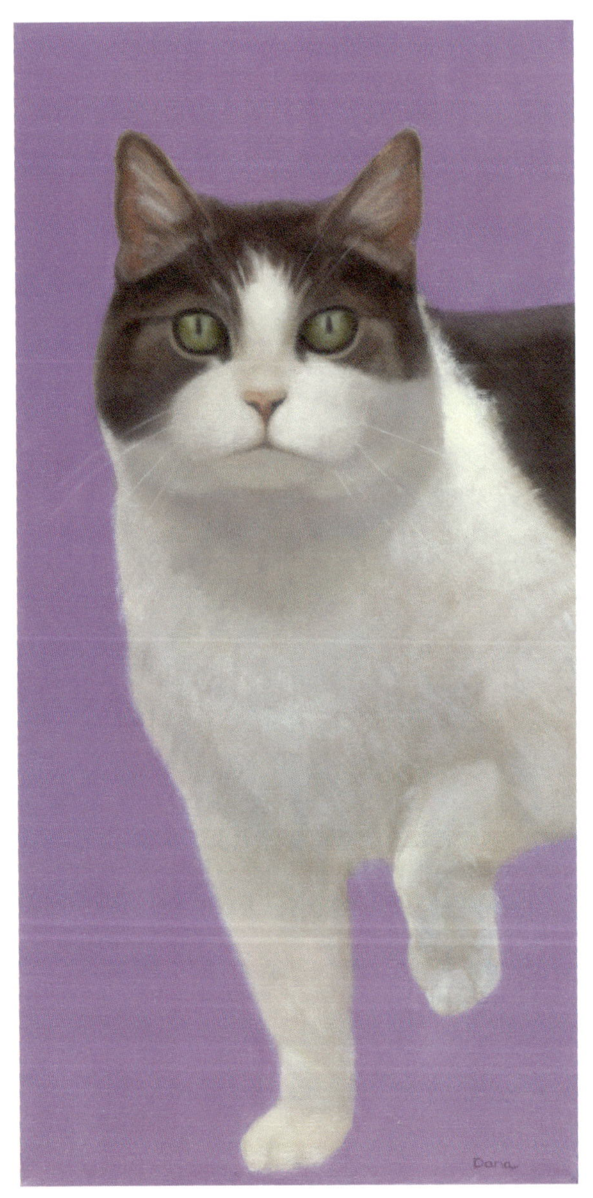

Conscientious Objector

I walk around
watching humans pass by
the things some of you do
make me want to cry

dismissing the fact
that kindness is defined
by the love in your heart
and the way that you act

stop calling yourself
an animal lover
while you continue to eat & wear
the life of another

you may look at me
and see just a cat
but I am your conscience
and that is that

It's Good to Be a Sheep

I have always been loved
It is how life should be
For all my animal friends
not for just me

A luckier sheep
I could not have been
my story is a good one
where do I begin?

My first human mama
she became ill
but she made sure my kin and me
went somewhere nice in her will

We arrived as a herd
at this magical farm
clearly the sanctuary motto
was first do no harm

I lived out my days
surrounded by beauty
and living in peace
was my only duty

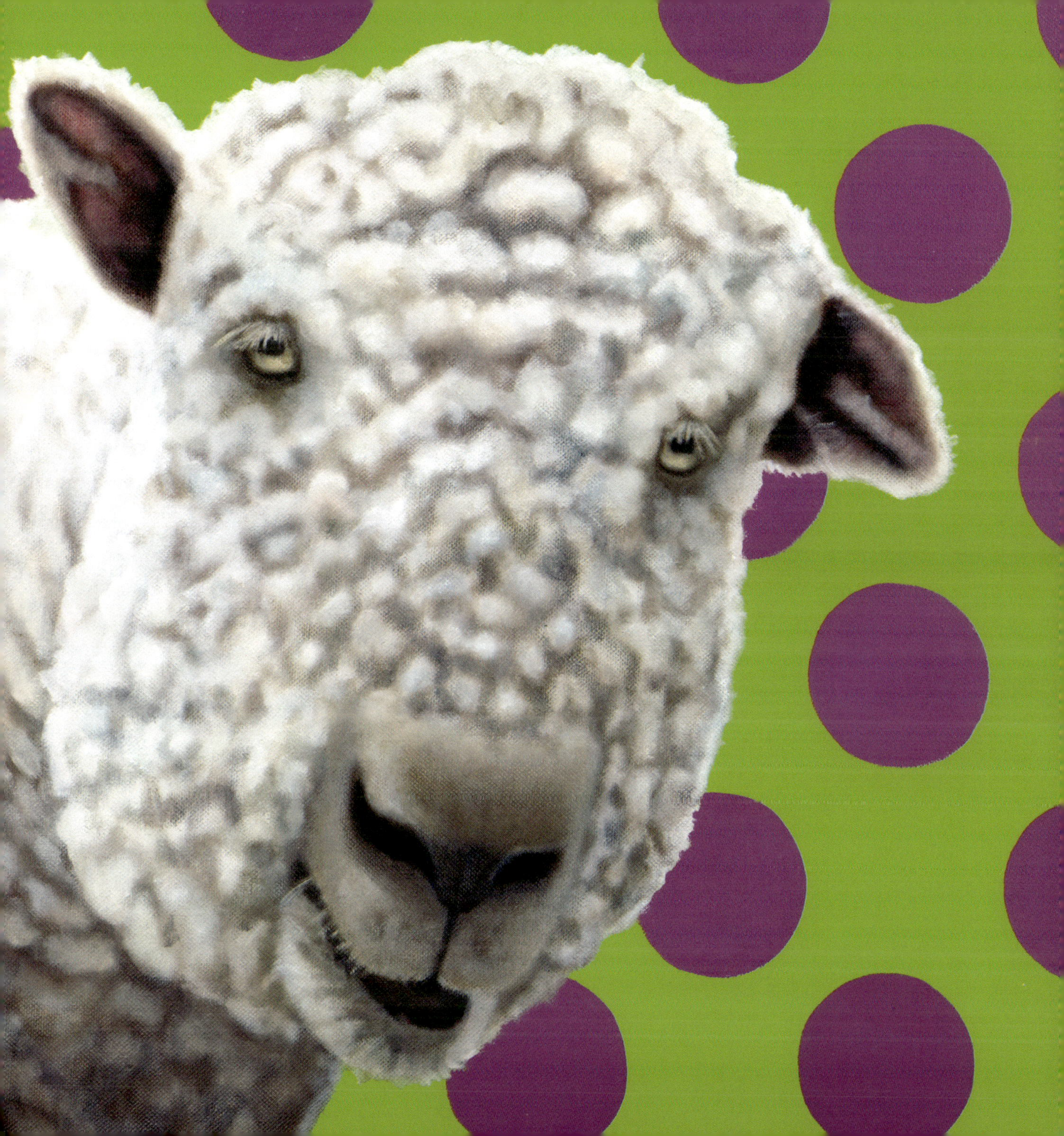

Eau de Human

donk-a-lonk-a-lee
donk-a-lonk-a-loo
how about a game
of peek-a-boo?

it isn't the same
as the game you may know
I look inside you and
your heart it shows

if it's honest and true
or somewhat askew
you realize I can tell
by the way that you smell

a love that is strong
can open all doors,
but a love that is not
it seeps out your pores

you think you can hide
underneath your clothes
but I can tell you for certain
a donkey always knows

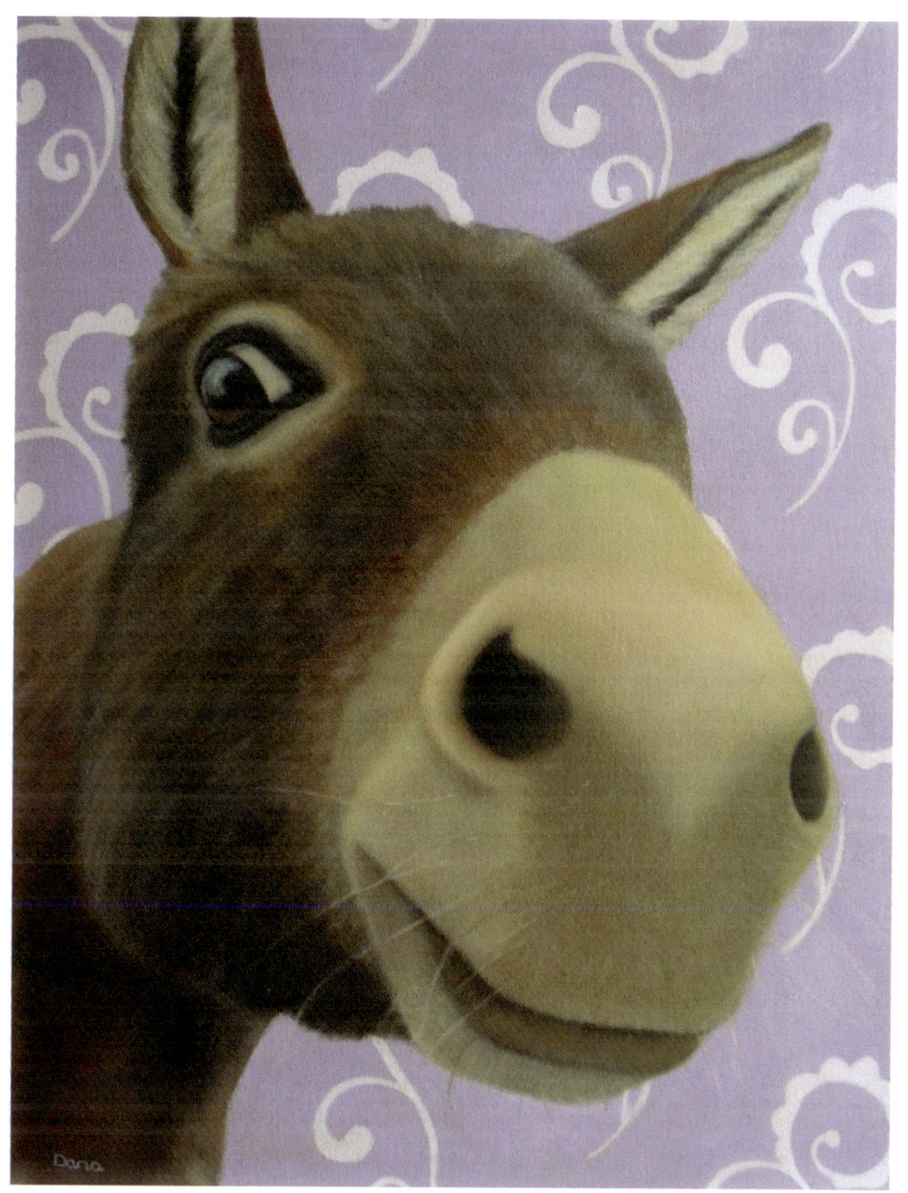

Dana

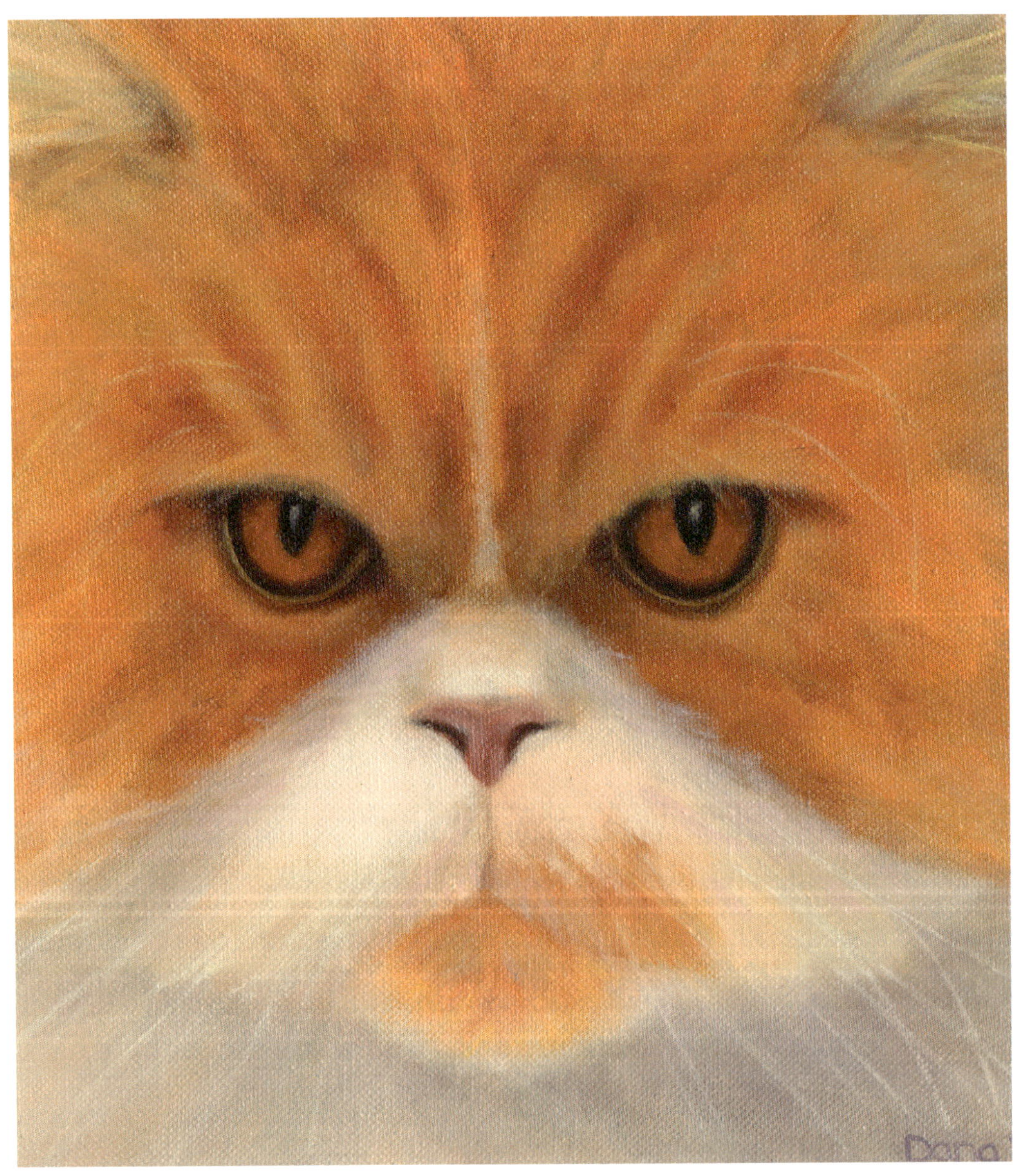

King of the Castle

I choose to sleep
in the kitchen sink
my personal throne
not as crazy as you think

seems everyone gathers
in this very room
nary a better spot
for my exquisite presence to loom

admired by all
who come for a snack
I really should charge
some sort of tax

clearly I landed
in just the right home
now would you be a dear
and fetch my mirror and comb?

The Hills Are Alive

I awaken the hills
with my melodic quack
for singing we ducks
have a god-given knack

Sure, Maria she had
a beautiful voice,
but most folks prefer mine
if given the choice

I can sing you a ditty
about queens and kings,
or would you rather hear
about my favorite things?

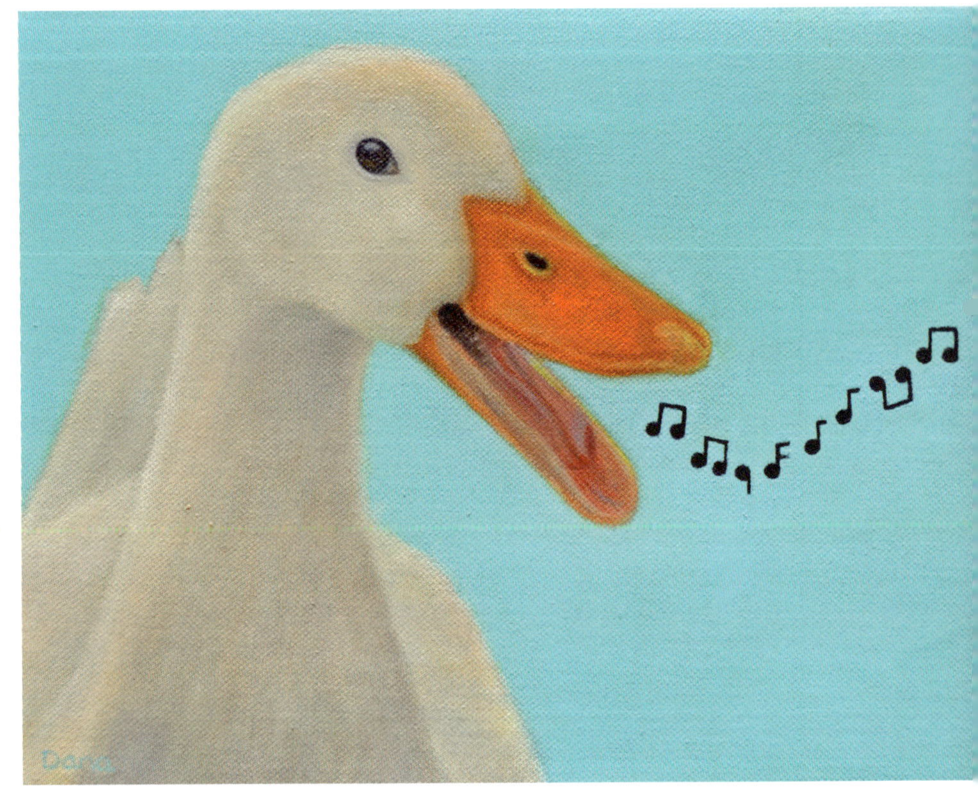

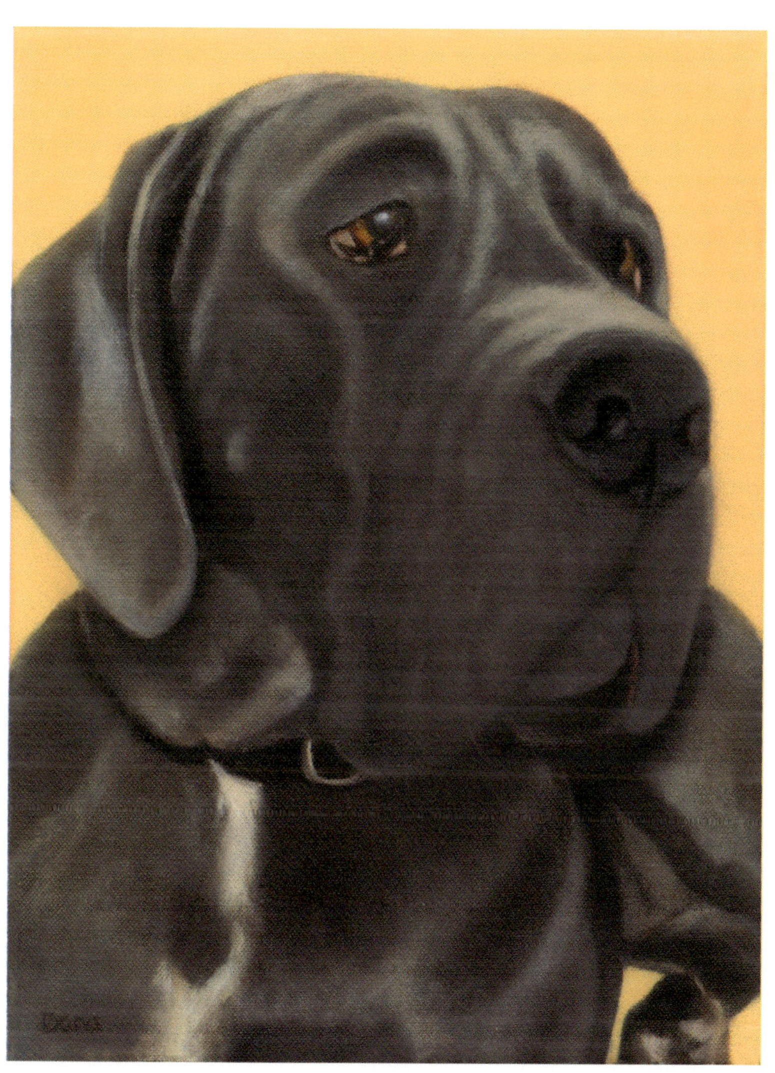

Velvet

The old song goes
that velvet's best worn blue,
but I doth protest.
Indeedy I do.

One look at my fur,
my body, my ears.
So lustrous, so soft.
Is it all coming clear?

Wear a shirt, or wear pants,
or a little pink dress,
for super smart dressing
you may have a knack.
But if you ask me,
the answer is clear.

The only way to wear velvet
is to wear classic black.

Close Talker

Prior to conversing
with people I meet,
you will find me rehearsing
the initial way that I greet.

I've been told some prefer
some space in the middle,
but I lean in close,
like a chin on a fiddle.

Bad breath not an issue,
never even a hint;
I keep right beside me
a fresh pack of Doublemint.

Come on, let's get cozy
and have a nice chat.
I like you up close;
what's wrong with that?

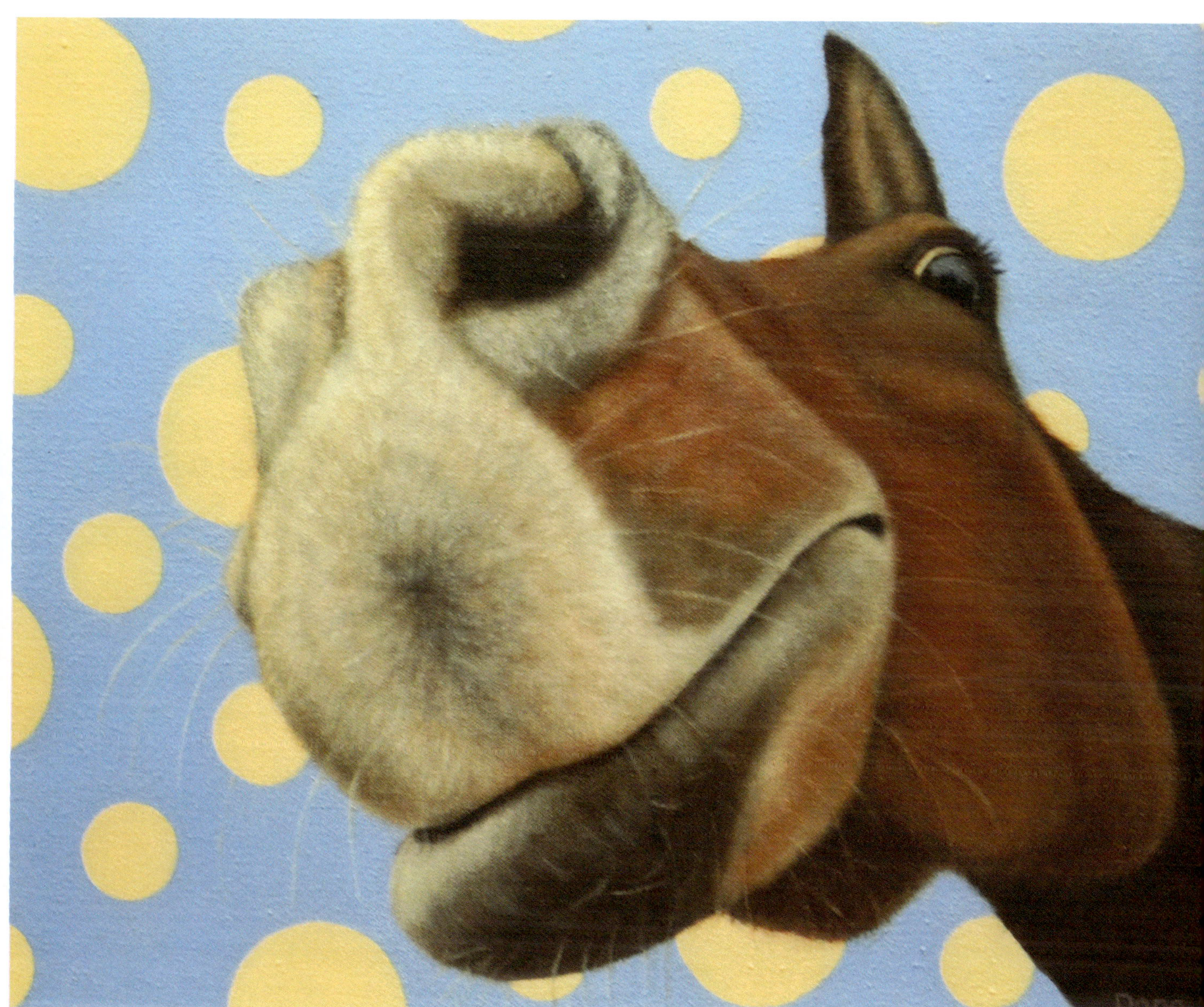

Sugar Rush

Just one lick, please;
that is all I will take.
I must have a taste
of that fluffy cupcake.

You think what I eat
is so green and lush.
But if I am being honest,
that grass tastes like mush.

I'm bigger than you,
and it's there for the taking.
But I will play fair;
after all,
you did the baking.

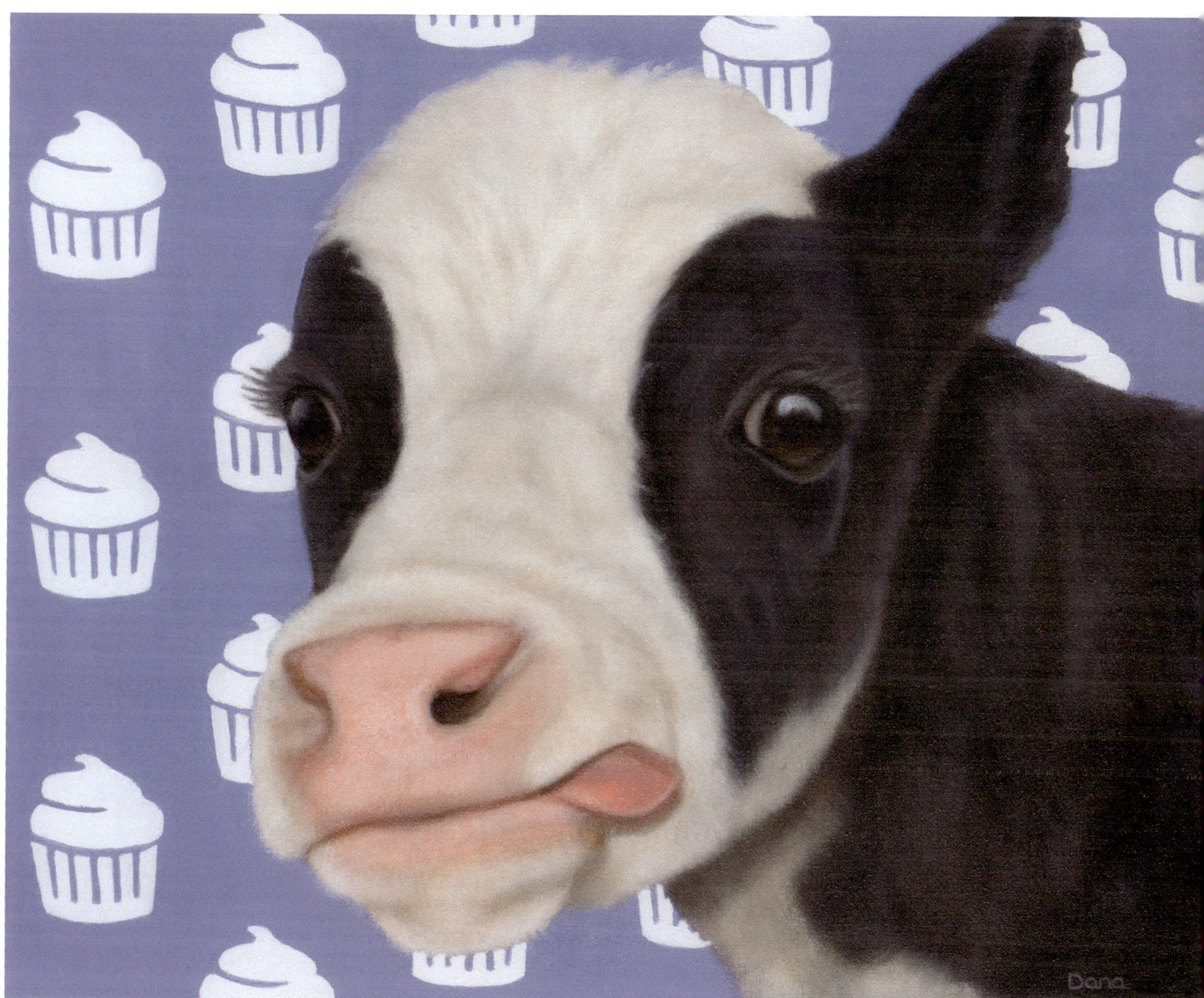

Dana

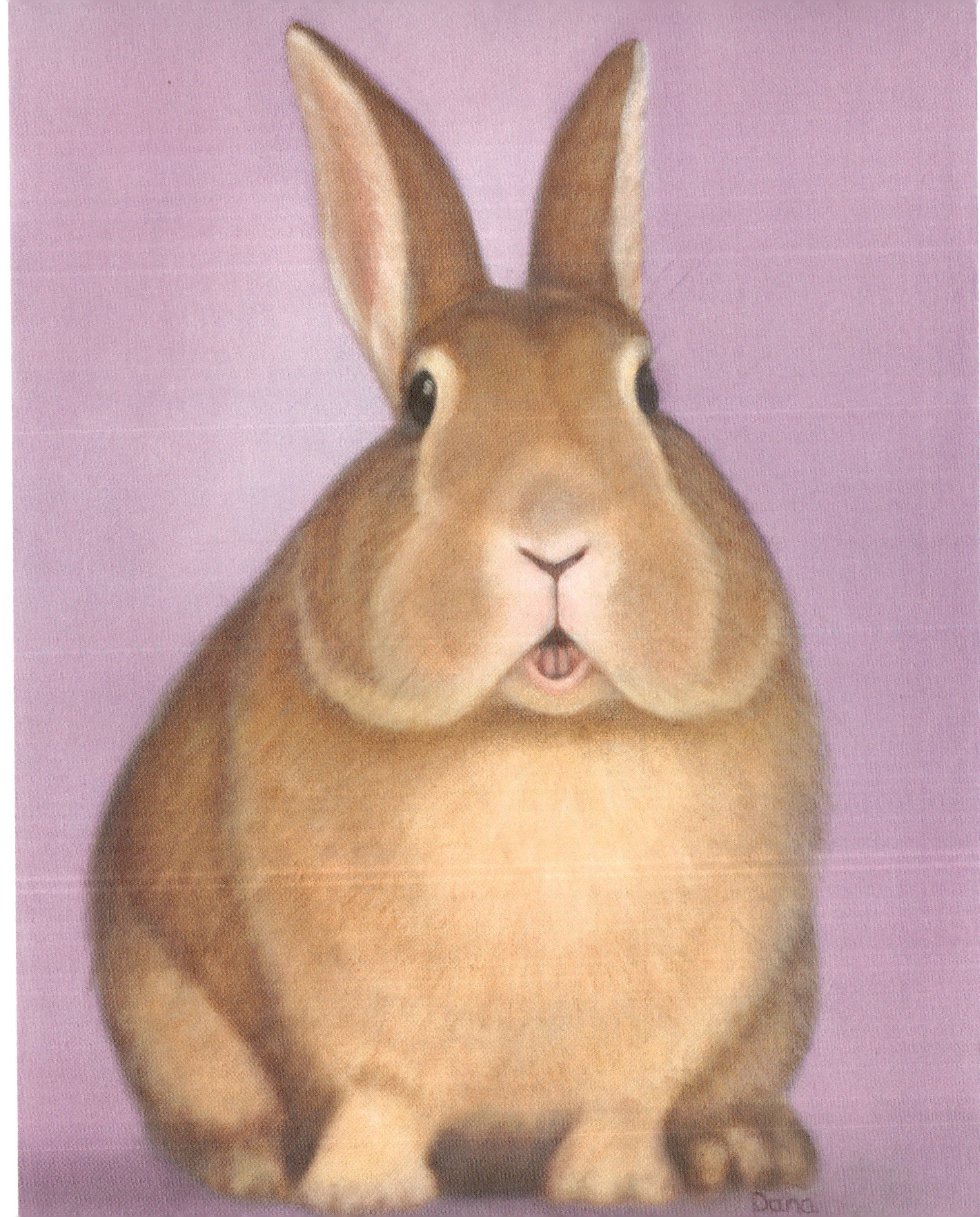
Dana

Let's Eat!

I nibble and gnaw
at things in my space
but when dinner time comes
I enjoy stuffing my face

I can fill them with hay
I can fill them with lettuce
I can fill them with carrots
all the above have their merits

You cannot resist
taking a peek
while I am enjoying the filling
of my gigantic sweet cheeks

Listen

I am looking at you
and asking you what?
What else can I do
except stare at your butt?

I sit on your table
like some living decor.
Can you even imagine
that my life is a bore?

How about a pond
with other fish friends?
Is this really how my life
both begins and ends?

A couple days later,
you answered my plea.
I see lily pads above
and a school of koi next to me.

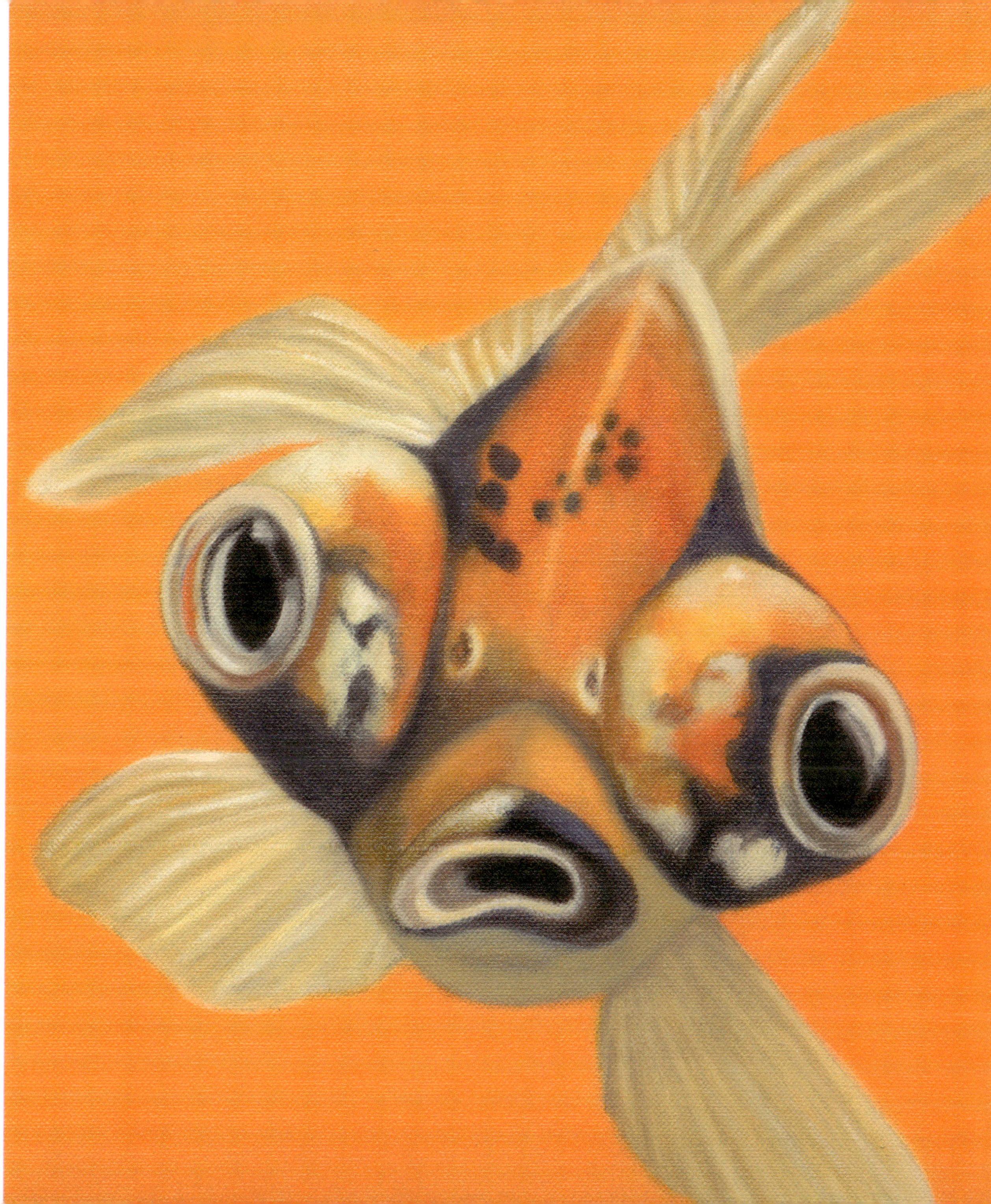

No fear of flying

My ears could be compared
to fuzzy propellers
much longer even
than the ears of Old Yeller

If I spin myself 'round
and get up off the ground
adventures will happen
the possibilities abound

I catch so much air
I fly over the mare
in the next pasture over
as she grazes on clover

I am everyone's hero
when I land on the ground
all my goat friends are stunned
none making a sound

They look on in awe
as I begin to sing
and am forever known as the goat
with the wind beneath my wings

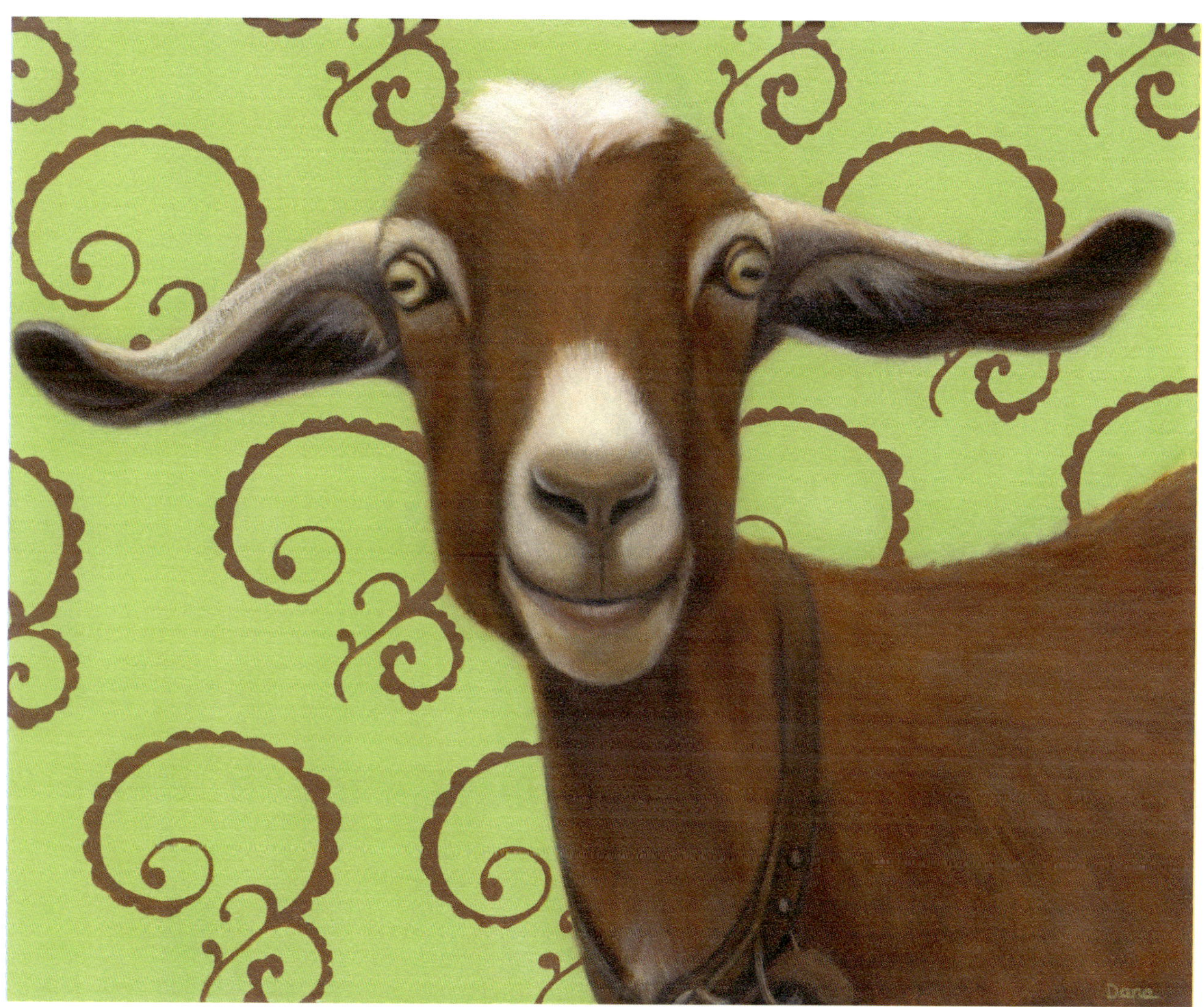

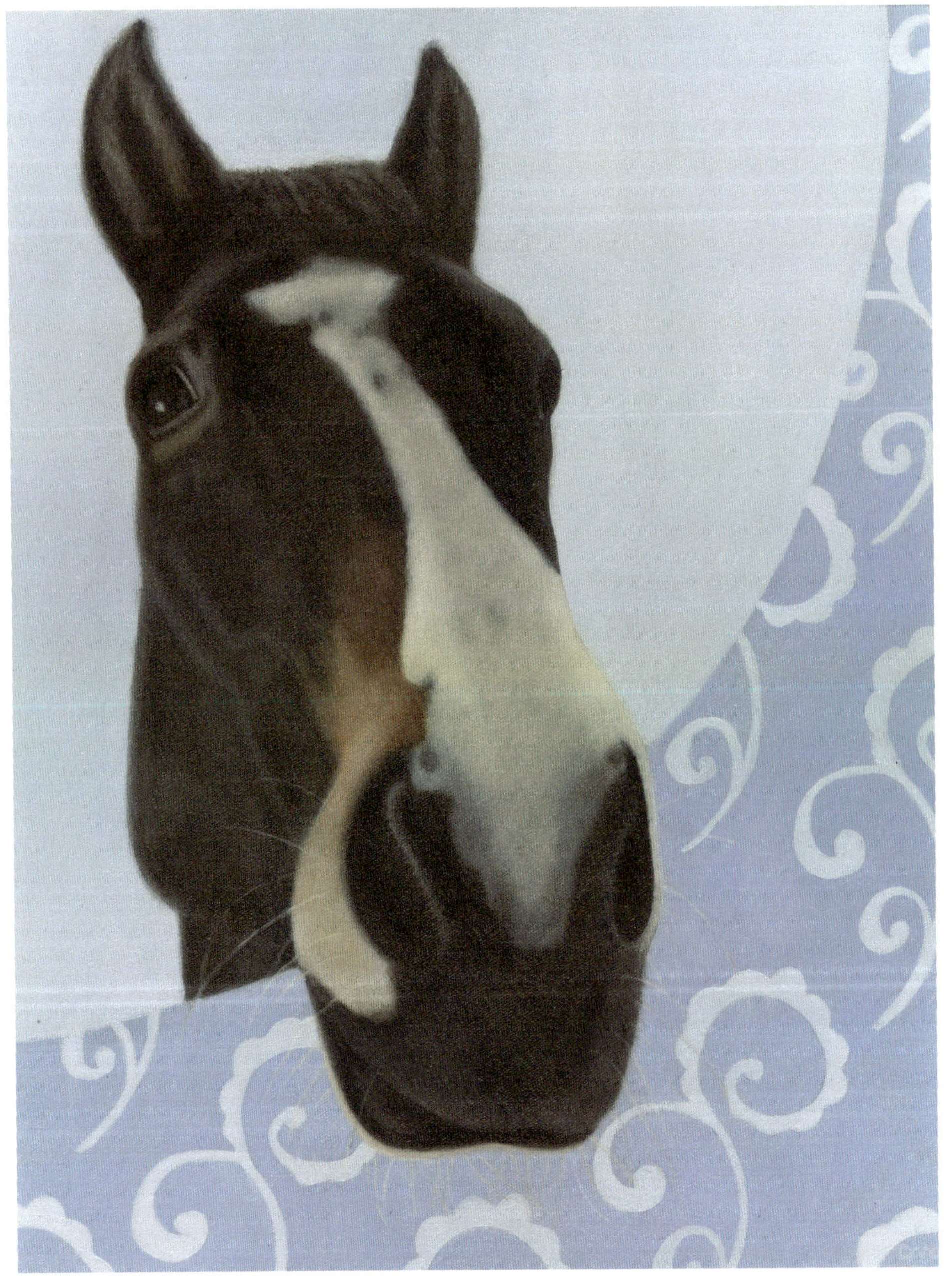

Perfect Sense

I can smell your love
I can taste your compassion
I can hear when you are near
I can sense when you feel fear

You show me such respect
You keep me warm and fed
You embrace every part of me
You know my eyes can't see

We will be friends forever
We have such fun together
We keep our hearts entwined
A stronger bond we could not find

Taking a Stand

I know it looks weird
when I kneel to eat.
I do this because
you neglected my feet.

We critters with hooves,
we need special care.
Go without a pedicure?
Ha! no human would dare.

If I had not been rescued
I wouldn't be walking,
never mind on this page
to do all this talking.

I speak for all hooves
with stern reprimand:
proper care is essential
for the cloven to stand.

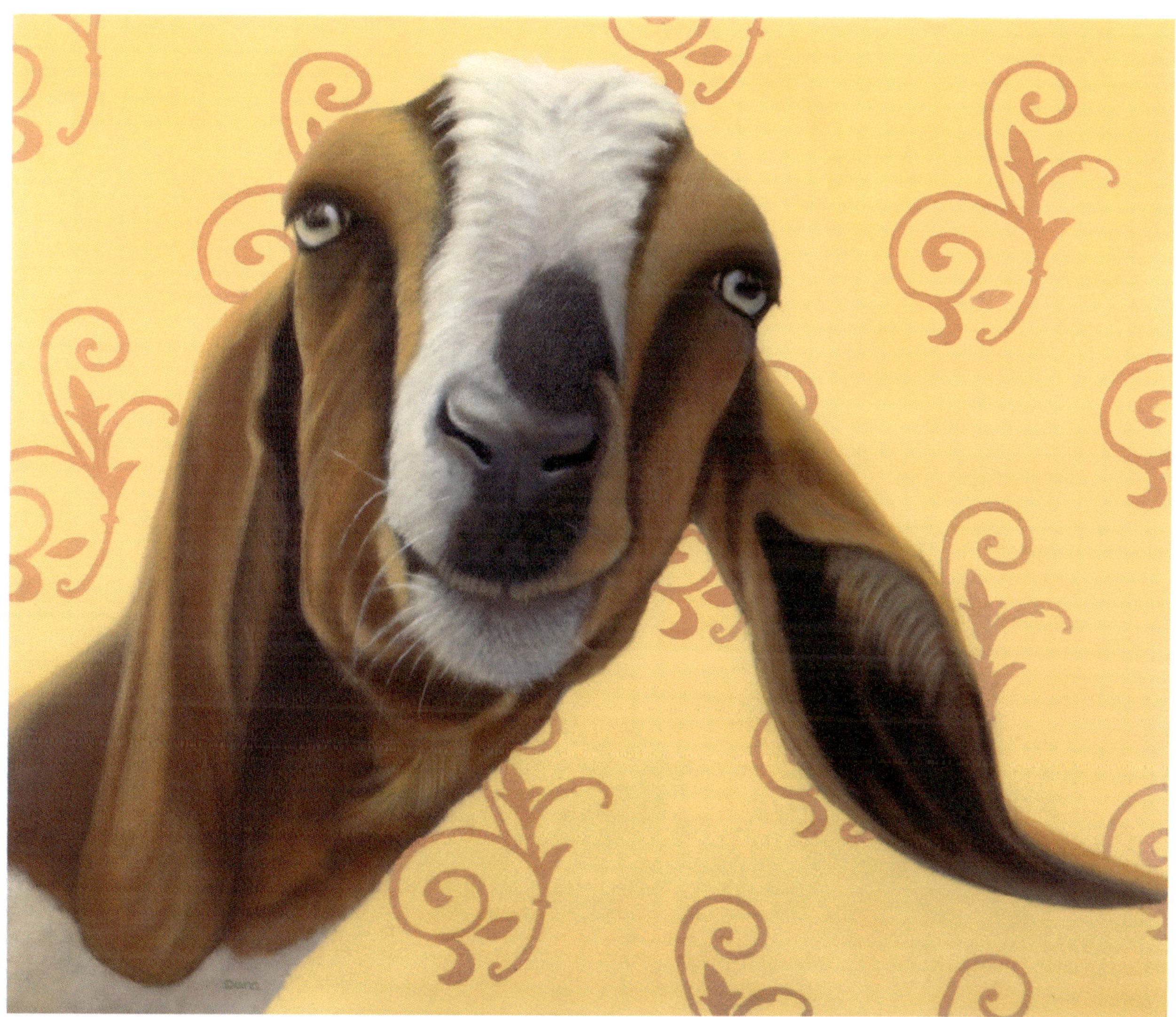

About the Animals: Selected Stories

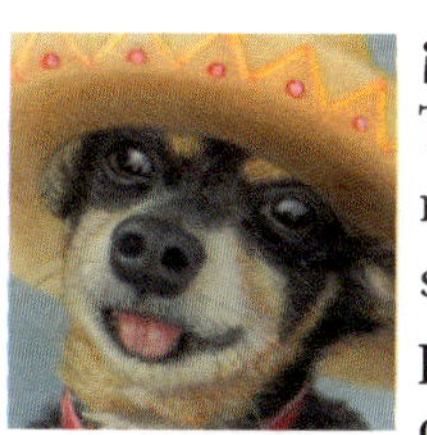

¡Ay Chihuahua!

This is a portrait of Sparky, an elderly Chihuahua/miniature pinscher mix from Sanctuary One in Jacksonville, Oregon. He was missing some teeth, so his tongue always hung out in this very cute way. This painting was created for Sanctuary One's annual fundraiser, which fell on Cinco de Mayo that year; images of his portrait were featured in table arrangements and on the invitation.

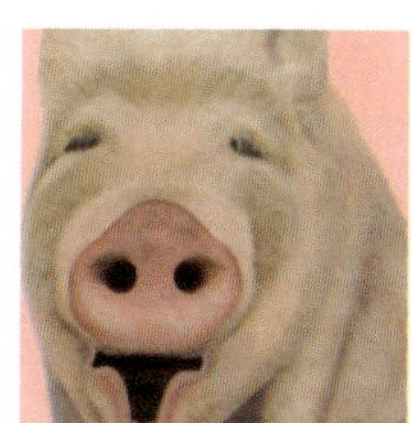

Lisa Laughs

Lisa was Sanctuary One's first ambassador pig, rescued from an abusive farmer by Whatcom Humane Society and transferred to Sanctuary One. There she lived out the remainder of her years, showered with attention. She was well known in the Rogue Valley, and Whatcom Humane Society created a short documentary about her, *Pigmalion: A Story in Three Acts*. This painting is shown at the very end of Lisa's film. The painting was based on a photograph taken by a volunteer in which Lisa was said to be talking, but Dana liked to think she was laughing, as Lisa ended up living quite the life.

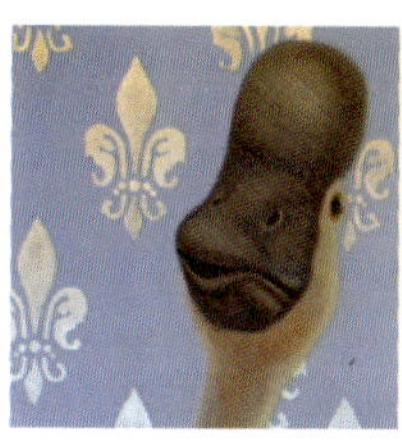

Maynard

Maynard was a Sanctuary One gander. He could be quite feisty but also had a softer side and a fondness for Sanctuary One's operations manager, Brian. He would hop up and sit in Brian's lap, showering him with love.

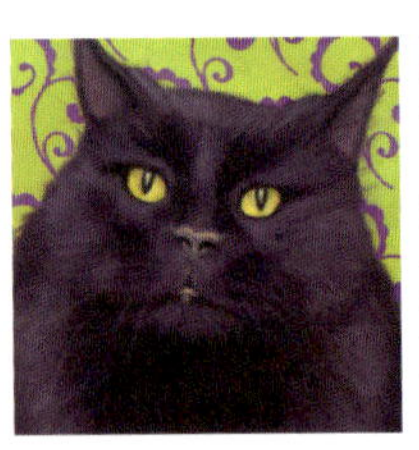

Poof!

This is a portrait of a ragtag black cat from the Jackson County Animal Shelter, based on a photograph taken by a volunteer. Dana made him look a bit fuller coated and renamed him "Poof!" like a magical black Halloween cat.

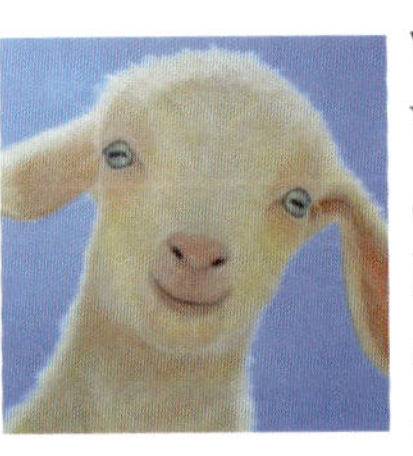

Violet

Violet was one of the last babies born at a former goat dairy farm. The owners were artisan cheese makers. However, they had a change of heart about their business and converted the dairy farm into an animal sanctuary—The Sanctuary at Soledad Goats. They now make artisan nut-based cheeses. One of their volunteers sent Dana a photograph of Violet, which inspired this painting.

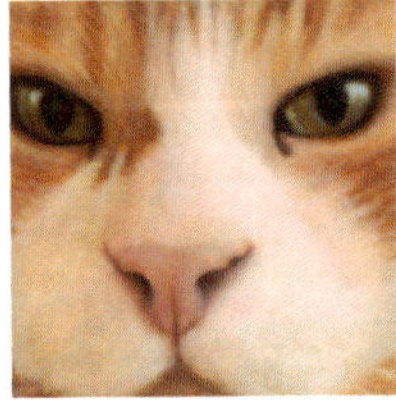

You Looking at Me?

Theo is a rescue cat who needed a special home because he does not get along with other animals (nor with most humans). He has been in a loving, one-cat home for the past seventeen years and is currently serving as general manager of Ashland Creek Press.

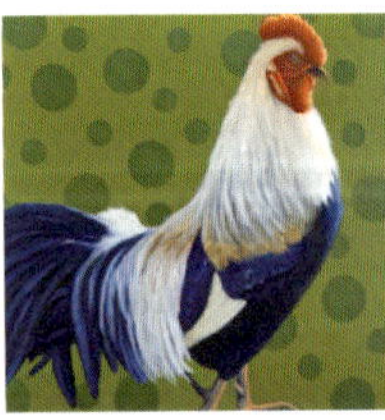

Captain Morgan

Morgan became a Sanctuary One rooster after appearing in the barnyard one day and acting as though he had always been there. It's unknown whether he was dropped off by someone, or whether he just walked or flew over to Sanctuary One. He was wonderful with his brood of chickens, making sure they were all safe.

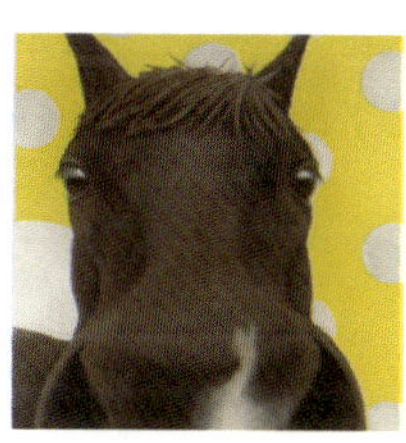

Chaps

Chaps is a Black Bay Moran/Arab Cross gelding from Equamore Horse Sanctuary in Ashland, Oregon. Chaps was surrendered in 2005 after severe neglect left him with an open, necrotic wound the size of a dinner plate on his left flank. After months of constant care at the sanctuary, Chaps fully recovered and now has only a scar.

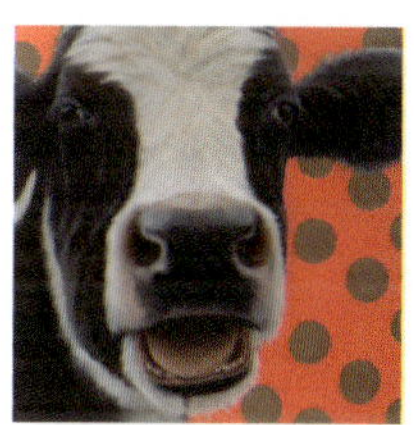

Cookies

Cookies came to Sanctuary One with her friend, Cream, from a veterinary college in California where she served as a blood donor. The sanctuary staff suspect that Cookies was a dairy cow prior to her days at the veterinary college, as she bonded very quickly with a new calf brought to Sanctuary One from Farm Sanctuary. She and the new calf, Holly, were adopted together to a family with other farm animals.

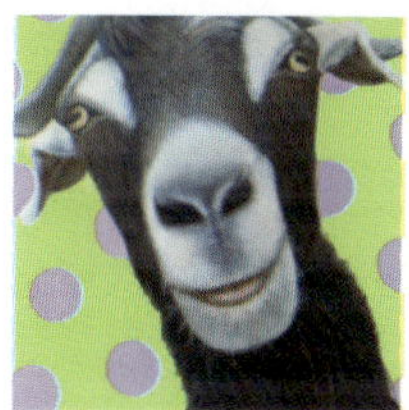

Django

Django spent most of his life chained to an oil barrel, which was moved from place to place as he grazed. Luckily for Django, a local animal activist rescued him and brought him to Sanctuary One. He is now integrated into the goat herd, living a normal goat life, surrounded with farm animal friends.

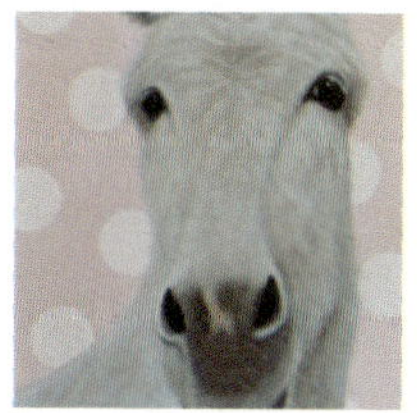

Bella II

As a young donkey, Bella lived on a small farm in Grants Pass, Oregon, and was used for roping practice. Once old enough to bear children, she was repeatedly doused with female horse urine (to entice a local stallion) and used to produce mules for sale. Once "used up," Bella was put on Craigslist and was purchased by another farm owner, who ended up leaving the state. Now Bella lives happily with Kat von Cupcake in Oregon's Applegate Valley, surrounded by another donkey, horses, goats, a dog, and a cat.

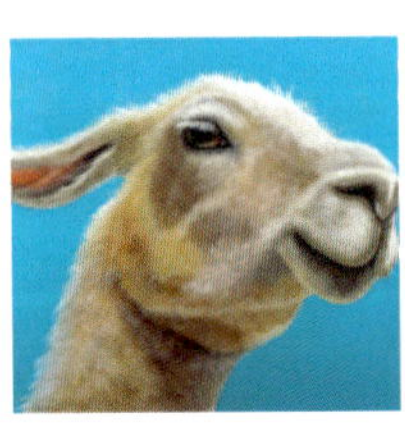

Ashley

Ashley is a beautiful white llama at Sanctuary One. Ashley came to the sanctuary with her mother, grandmother, and aunt; their owner was trying to get out of a bad situation and couldn't take them with her. Ashley is the largest of her family and quite confident, strolling around the pasture as if she owns everything in it.

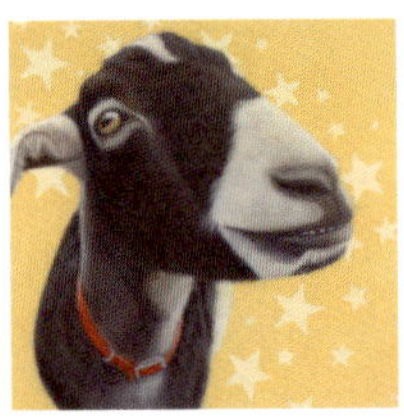

A Star Is Born

Orville was a friendly Nubian goat from Sanctuary One. He and his brother Wilbur came to the sanctuary when their family moved to Hawaii and could not bring them along. From the sanctuary, they were adopted to a wonderful home, where Orville lived out the rest of his life.

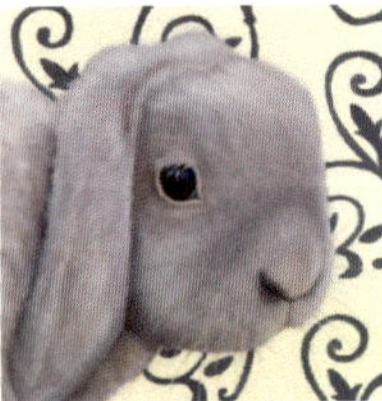

Chive

Chive was the first of Dana's many adopted bunnies; he had been discovered alone at a local park. Chive was an older bun, requiring a lot of medical and dental care, but he was Dana's first studio bunny and a big presence in the studio. He passed away after only two short years with Dana, but his bonded partner, Chelsea, and another bunny from the shelter, Nell, still live in the art studio.

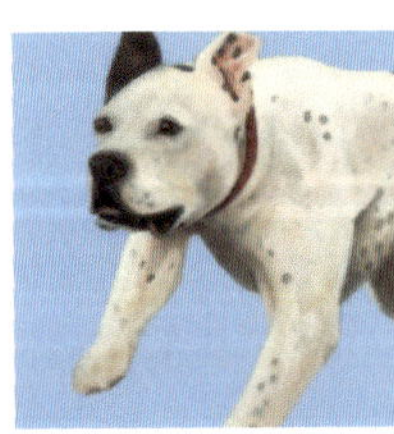

It's Riley's Ball

In this portrait, based on a photograph, Dana's adopted pit pull, Riley, is in mid-air chasing his ball at the dog park. Because it looked like he was flying, reminding Dana of the old *Underdog* television series, when she painted him, she used a sky-blue background instead of the green grassy background that was actually there.

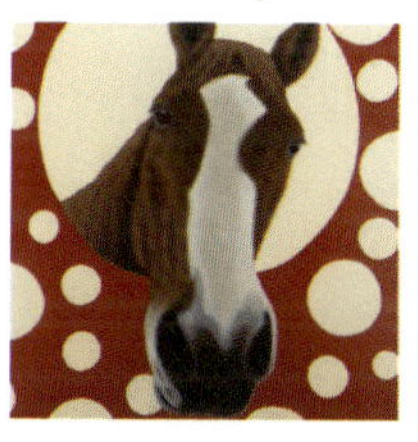

Kizzy in Reflection

Kizzy is a chestnut quarter horse mare from Equamore Horse Sanctuary. Kizzy had multiple owners and was finally surrendered in 2011 because she could not be ridden. Her legs are bowed, which causes her to collapse under the weight of the saddle and rider. Kizzy was also malnourished and in need of serious dental care. She is now fully retired with a herd of three other mares and a gelding friend. This painting is titled "Kizzy in Reflection" because Dana flipped the image in Photoshop, not realizing that her markings would be reversed—so, this is how Kizzy sees herself!

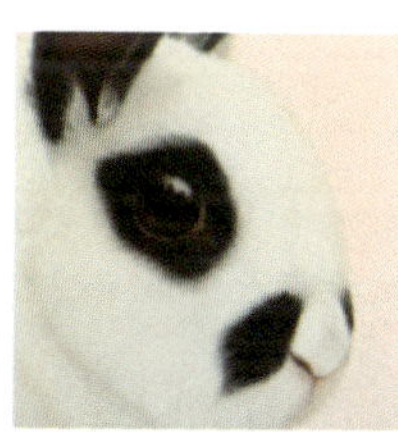

Nell

Nell was at the Jackson County Animal Shelter when Dana noticed she had been there for more than a month and spent most of the time hiding, so no one could see her. When Dana brought Nell home to foster her, Nell could barely hop around, as her legs had atrophied. She is now healthy and happy—and Dana has since adopted her.

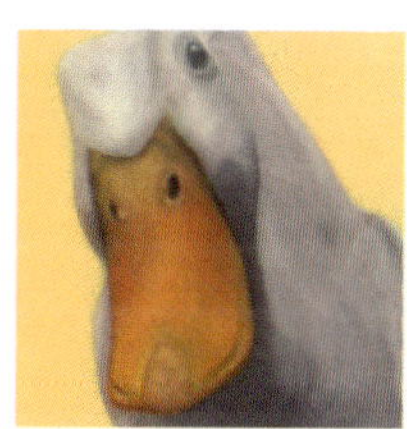

Peeking Pekin

Ping is a Pekin duck from Sanctuary One. Ping came to Sanctuary One from Farm Sanctuary in Orland, California, along with his Pekin friends Mr. Dandy, Reginald, Fillmore, Dudley, Francis, and Ducky. They were all in good health and now share the sanctuary's duck pond with Canada geese who come and go as they please.

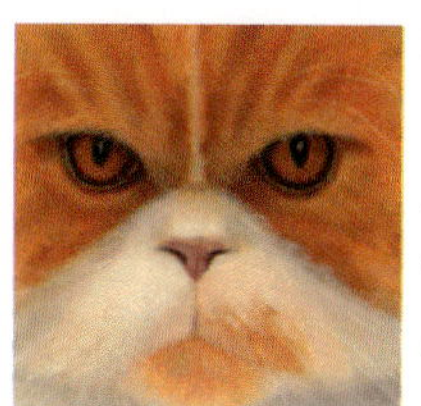

Sid with Attitude

Sid is a Persian cat who was up for adoption at the Jackson County Animal Shelter at the time Dana completed this painting, based on a volunteer photograph. Sid had been returned to the shelter more than once because of his very large personality, but fortunately, with his last placement, Sid found doting parents with no other pets who allow him to rule the house and sleep in the bathroom sink.

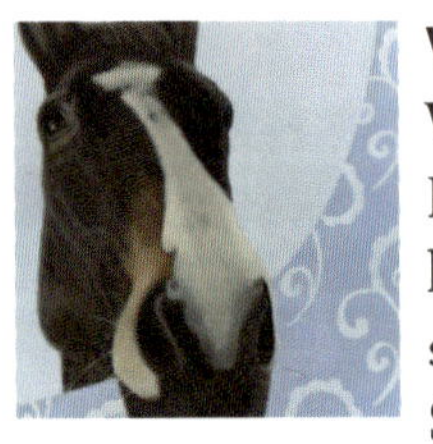

Wishes

Wishes is a beautiful blind mustang mare who found her way to Equamore Horse Sanctuary in 2012 via Shane, an elderly paint horse who was her guide for many years. At the sanctuary, Wishes and Shane shared side-by-side stalls and spent time together in the indoor arena. Sadly, Shane died six weeks after coming to the sanctuary—yet around the same time, thoroughbred Eddie went blind from an untreatable eye condition. In the safety of the indoor arena by day and their side-by-side stalls at night, Wishes and Eddie became friends, and Equamore created a special field for them. The two have memorized the field's dimensions and can be seen galloping, grazing, and grooming each other—all of the things sighted horses do.

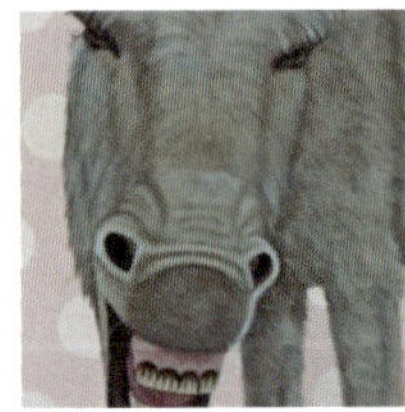

Little Inez

Little Inez came to Sanctuary One through Strawberry Mountain Mustangs Rescue; she was in a hoarding situation and had never been handled. She had a severe skin infection on her face and was emaciated. When Kat saw her photo on the Sanctuary One website, she hightailed it to the sanctuary to adopt her as a companion for Bella. Because Little Inez was extraordinarily timid, it took more than three months to gain her trust—but now she is the friendliest animal in Kat's herd.

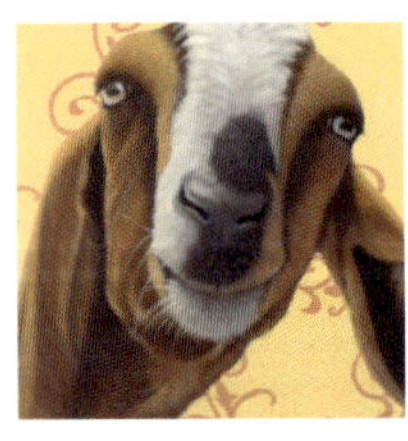

Winkin

Winkin is a Boer goat from Sanctuary One and the mother of Blinkin, rescued as part of a thirty-goat herd due to severe neglect. Winkin has a malformed foot, which is a result of poor hoof care before her rescue, but she seems to get along just fine. Winkin and Blinkin are very bonded, each crying out if the other is not within sight.

Acknowledgments

The artwork included in this book was painted from reference photos taken by Dana Feagin, her fellow volunteers, and other creative people who allowed Dana to paint from their images. Two professional photographers who allowed the use of their images as reference material deserve credit for their awesome photography: Brooke Turner, a photographer for the Jackson County Animal Shelter (pages 44 and 86), and Justine Johnson, a wedding photographer based in Portland, Maine (page 13).

The poems "Change Is Good," "Goat Power," and "no joyrides" first appeared in the anthology *Even In My Dreams*, edited by Emma Letessier.

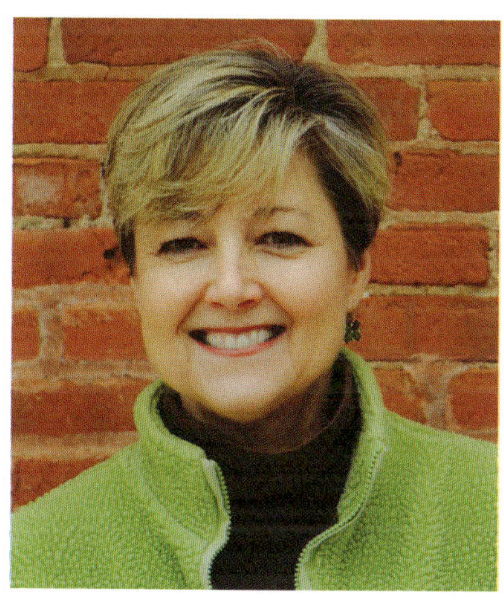

About the Artist

Dana Feagin is an oil painter based in Ashland, Oregon, and uses her art to raise money for animal charities. Dana is a board member for Sanctuary One, a volunteer for Friends of the Animal Shelter (FOTAS), and an artist member with HeARTsSpeak—a global community of artists, shelter staff, rescue volunteers, and animal advocates working together to ensure that no shelter animal goes unseen. Dana is also a mom to four former shelter dogs and two adopted bunnies. For more information, visit Dana's website at www. danafeagin.com.

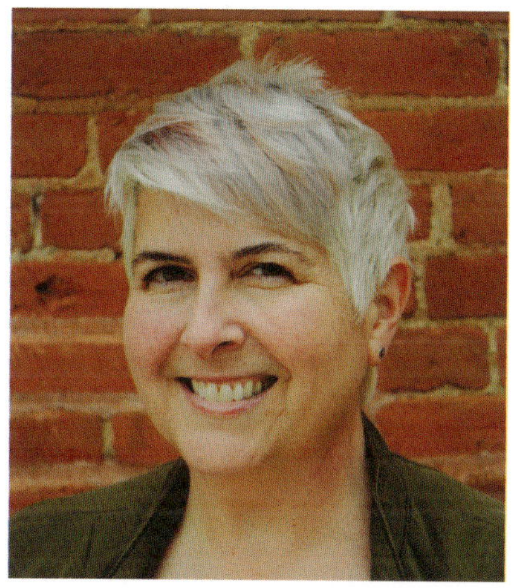

About the Poet

Kat von Cupcake spent her pre-retirement years working as a San Francisco police officer. During her eight years in the K9 Unit, she realized the extraordinary intelligence and capabilities that animals possess. Her appreciation for animals and desire for the space to expand her understanding and love for other species landed her in Southern Oregon. Now Kat bakes compassionate treats for humans and donates her profits to animal charities, tends to her own herd of rescued critters, and sits on the board of directors for Sanctuary One.

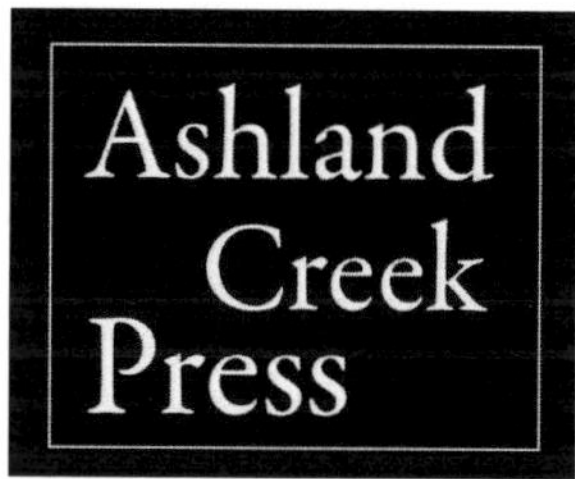

About the Publisher

Ashland Creek Press is an independent, vegan-owned publisher of ecofiction, which includes books in all genres about animals, the environment, and the planet we all call home. We are passionate about books that foster an appreciation for worlds outside our own, for nature and the animal kingdom, and for the ways in which we all connect. To learn more, visit us at www.AshlandCreekPress.com.

CPSIA information can be obtained at www.ICGtesting.com
Printed in the USA
BVIW12n0027010317
477443BV00001B/2